THE
Seer's House

❖

The Seer's House

First Published 1997
© Copyright 1997 James McConnell and John McCreedy

AMBASSADOR PRODUCTIONS LTD,
Providence House
16 Hillview Avenue,
Belfast, BT5 6JR
Northern Ireland

Emerald House,
1 Chick Springs Road, Suite 206
Greenville,
South Carolina 29609
United States of America

THE
Seer's House

— ❖ —

THE REMARKABLE STORY OF
JAMES McCONNELL
AND THE
WHITEWELL METROPOLITAN TABERNACLE

— ❖ —

JOHN McCREEDY

AMBASSADOR

BELFAST ◆ **GREENVILLE**
NORTHERN IRELAND   SOUTH CAROLINA

Dedication

*This book is dedicated to
my Pastor, James McConnell,
who led me to the Lord.*

Acknowledgements

Let me say a word of thanks to the following people:
*My friend **Stephen Hill**. You have taught me that God prefers faithfulness
to success. I thank you for that.*
***Maureen Hill** - you gave me so many books to read I thought I would
write one myself, Maureen. God bless.*
***Margaret Hillis**, who, when I was homeless and hungry, took me in and
fed me. God bless.*
***Noel Davidson**, senior editor with Ambassador, who added a touch of
class. Thank you.*
***Tom and Isobel Martin** - you are my friends. I love you both.*
***Paul Malcolmson** - for his constant encouragement. Thank you, brother.*
***Stuart McCullough** - my technical advisor. A big thank you.*
***Tommy Braden** - A good Shepherd and friend. Thank you for helping me
believe I could do this.*
***Stephen Hamilton**, our photographer, for his tireless work.*
*Last but certainly not least - a massive thank you to my proof reader,
Jackie Davidson. Simply the best.*

CONTENTS

❖

❖ PART THREE - FILLED WITH WISDOM

❖ PART FOUR - AND THE GRACE OF GOD WAS UPON HIM

❖ A SERMON BY DR. JAMES MCCONNELL

FOREWORD

❖

In any walk of life, James McConnell would have been a great success. In any job he would have risen to the very top; he could have been a prosperous businessman. There is nothing mediocre in his personality.

Born in humble surroundings, humbly speaking, his future prospects looked bleak. It seemed that adverse conditions would consign him to a nondescript life.

However, at an early age he demonstrated a work ethic, a friendly but determined spirit that gave strong indicators that this was no ordinary young man. His industry, enthusiasm, positive attitude and refusal to accept the "status quo" pointed to an outstanding tomorrow.

Early on in life he gave his life to Christ and the Christian world can thank God that his energies were not challenged into the commercial and material world but into the Kingdom of God. From his conversion his attributes were not to be dedicated to making a name for himself but to exalt his Lord and Saviour and make His name glorious.

This is the history of a humble, unassuming man who has achieved excellence in God's work. A story that will make you laugh and make you cry. It will inspire and challenge you. It will stimulate your faith to want to do great things for God. It will encourage and motivate you to achieve the purposes of God in your life. It will make you determined that you will not die until, like James McConnell, you have fulfilled God's destiny for your life.

This man's ministry started with ten people in Whitewell Orange Hall. Today over 7,000 people attend meetings every week in their beautiful new church. It is indeed a modern-day miracle, a 20th century demonstration of the power, life and vitality of the Holy Spirit, which was in the life of the "Early Church".

James McConnell is a great man of God. A man of faith and prayer. A man moving in the miraculous dimensions of the Holy Spirit. He is an outstanding preacher and communicator. He is also a man of the people. Success has not made him aloof. He is very approachable, his door always open to all and sundry. Young children and teenagers love him.

We thank God for James and his wife Margaret, wonderful people! It is one of life's great joys and privileges to know them.

May the remaining years of his ministry be even more glorious than the first forty.

Rev Wynne Lewis
General Superintendent Elim Pentecostal Churches

PREFACE

'THE SEER'S HOUSE'

❖

"Then Saul drew near to Samuel in the gate, and said, Tell me, I pray thee where the seer's house is. And Samuel answered Saul, and said, I am the seer: go up before me unto the high place; for ye shall eat with me today, and tomorrow I will let thee go, and will tell thee all that is in thine heart." I Samuel 9:18-19

To my surprise I discovered Chambers Dictionary's definition of a 'Seer' to be - a man who sees, or forsees. In ancient Israel, recorded in I Samuel 8:9, before Prophets were officially recognised, those with the prophetic spirit were quaintly called 'Seers' ... They were men specially gifted and anointed by the Holy Spirit to see more than the average man saw.

Now I certainly do not profess to be a Prophet or even a Seer. However, like many sincere servants of God, there have been times and moments when my eyes have seen more clearly things, events, people, which to the outward appearance looked normal, natural and sometimes even drastic ... but the anointed eye sees far more.

Just like Elisha prayed for his young attendant at the city of Dothan in II Kings 6:17, when they were surrounded by the Syrian army, the young man cried, "Alas, my Master! how shall we do?" Elisha prayed, "Lord open his eyes". To the young man's amazement he saw the mountain covered by glistening, angelic horsemen and chariots of fire.

That's why this book is entitled, The Seer's House! The story of James McConnell and The Whitewell Metropolitan Tabernacle began on 23rd February, 1957.

It has been my privilege to be in charge of this one great church for forty years. The story of Whitewell, The Metropolitan Tabernacle, is unique in this sense, that its Pastor and its people began on the same day. During those years one observes a lot, one learns a lot and one fails a lot. I feel that after all these years in a long pastorate I have something to give and tell, if people will give me a hearing.

I am convinced, like many Bible students, that not only are we living in the last days but we are living in the last of the last days. The last days began when the Lord Jesus commenced His earthly ministry ... Matthew 4:17 and Hebrews 1:1-3. Now nearly 2,000 years later, we are in the last of the last days. Time is short!

There is one characteristic of last times - for example, the last Judge in Israel was blind Samson, the last King of Judah was blind Zedekiah and the last church of the New Testament, Laodicea, was blind. It seems, in these days of crisis, in our beloved province of Ulster and in Great Britain, that the nation's spiritual leaders are blind. They don't seem to be able to perceive or ascertain the real plight and needs of the people nor how to meet those needs. Now I sincerely hope that this Pastor is not blind nor the church he is leading.

I could never have written this book, I have too many commitments - preaching daily and looking to God for messages to bring to the people. It took Mr. Sam Lowry of Ambassador Productions Ltd. to encourage me to think about it and my young colleague John McCreedy to write it, and Mr. Noel Davidson from Ambassador, a sincere child of God, to make all this possible. I thank each of them for their encouragement.

If through the reading of this book God will anoint and inspire some servant of His to do greater things for His Kingdom, then it will have been worthwhile. I hereby send this book with a prayer that there will be many "Seer's Houses" throughout this nation.

Dr. James McConnell
February, 1997

INTRODUCTION

❖

D uring years of dedicated service to his church at
Whitewell, Pastor James McConnell has preached
thousands of sermons packed with sentences he
describes as 'one liners.'

None, however, reveal the clarity of vision regarding his
own personal calling more than, "If God has called you to
preach, then don't stoop to become Prime Minister."

It was a comment made during the heat of an address and
was never meant to be insulting to the leader of our nation. On
the contrary, the pastor was emphasising the point, "If God has
called you to preach the gospel - then preach that gospel. Don't
get bogged down in the things of the world, no matter how
important they appear to be."

Certainly this rugged, but respected pastor, learned early
in life how to put God first in all things. Like his boyhood hero,
Charles Hadden Spurgeon, the call of God came to Pastor
McConnell while still only a child. Yet even at that early period
of his life there were obvious indications of that decisiveness of

character and boldness of address he has become renowned for.

Other similarities exist between the two, such as being brought up by foster parents, receiving striking prophecies as young men, displaying great fortitude in their characters and the building of the Metropolitan Tabernacles in London and Belfast respectively, to name but a few.

Early comparisons with the nineteenth century preacher Spurgeon are evident, particularly in relation to the reading of books. In his account of Spurgeon's life, Arnold Dallimore records that Charles was still a child when he became aware of Christian books. So too was the young James, who learned to read theology at an early age.

In recent years James McConnell has been discussed by evangelicals from various backgrounds. Few people, however, fully understand his person and his character. Many of his congregation admit that they don't really know him.

Apart from the book, 'Light on a Hill', written by the pastor in 1987, there has been no appropriate biography. In this particular account of his life I will try to portray his true character, while uncovering the real motivation behind his burning desire to see precious souls surrender their lives to the Lord Jesus Christ.

They say there was only one Charles Spurgeon. To his modern-day congregation, there is only one James McConnell, who says he would like to be remembered as being very much his own man and a man who loved the Lord Jesus Christ.

And finally ...

Having completed this book, I can relate more fully to the words of a man who once described a career in journalism:

"It will kill you in the end, but it will keep you alive while you are at it."

I know what he means.

"And the Lord answered me and said, Write the vision and make it plain upon tables, that he may run that readeth it." Habakkuk 2:2

John McCreedy
1997

PART ONE

AND THE CHILD GREW

Chapter One

BORN AND BORN AGAIN

❖

Edward McConnell worked in the shipyard. He was one of 20,000 employees and was known as a 'driller.' Belfast's massive shipyard, Harland and Wolff, dominated the skyline of East Belfast in the 1930's and was one of the city's major employers.

It was in the east of the city that Edward met Jean Anderson and they married and set up home at Spring Street.

On 15th May, 1937, their son, James, was born into that humble home.

Young James's earliest memories of those days were of his attendance at two places; one was for his education, the other was to lead ultimately to his salvation.

At age five he started school at Nettlefield Primary School. It was formal teaching and large classes, but the young pupil was taught how to respect authority.

The other place he attended was the Iron Hall. His mother, though not a Christian, insisted that he come with her every Sunday evening to the service. On one memorable evening, the speaker was a Welsh preacher named Towell Evans. The man was a fiery evangelist who spoke with tremendous conviction. A sense of God pervaded the place.

As the congregation filed out the evangelist stopped James and his mother at the door. As he shook James's mother's hand he said to her earnestly, "Jeanie, it's time to get right with the Lord."

Although his mother didn't respond initially, those words left a mark on her and on young James.

As well as going to the evening service with his mother, he also attended Sunday School each week.

James went happily. He enjoyed the friendship of other boys in his class, but there was another reason. He really longed to be saved.

For months James had paid acute attention to Christian matters, although whether he was conscious of this at the time is debatable. He knew there was a heaven and a hell. What he didn't understand then was how to receive salvation, so he remained burdened in his spirit.

Approaching the age of seven he was transferred to a new class, taught by a young man called Sammy Jamison. At that time the teacher was only eighteen years of age, a faithful young Christian who was to play a major role in the life of James McConnell.

One particular Sunday afternoon James listened intently. The things that Sammy Jamison said convinced him as a young boy of his need of Christ. He had been thinking about giving his life to Jesus Christ for a while, but whatever his teacher said that day persuaded him there was no time to waste.

After the Sunday School was dismissed he stayed behind, pulled the teacher aside, and said, "Mr. Jamison, I want to come to the Lord."

Many might have overlooked such a request from a young child, but Sammy Jamison was wise enough not to make little of the request. On the contrary, he knelt the young child down at an old bench and explained the way of salvation simply to him as he had done many times before in the Sunday School class.

At that moment young James McConnell embraced Christ with all his heart. Despite his tender years he fully understood the words, "Except a man be born again, he cannot see the Kingdom of God." John 3:3.

He had not only heard but believed the truth that Jesus was his Saviour.

It was to prove a momentous decision. His religious apathy had been blown apart. From the moment of his conversion he was consumed by a desire to achieve something special for God.

Sammy Jamison didn't neglect this young convert. He was one of the first to recognise in young James a potential for God, and spent many years encouraging this new child in the faith.

James discovered that not only did he receive a Saviour that day in the Iron Hall, he received a Father as well.

He was shielded from sickness and disease, but more importantly he was comforted by the fellowship that he had with his new-found Heavenly Father.

Through reading the Bible and praying to God constantly, both in his little room in Spring Street and under the trees in Ormeau Park, he obtained spiritual solace and developed spiritual strength.

Chapter Two

AND THE CHILD GREW

❖

James McConnell's family survived the war, but not the
illnesses, which back then had plagued more than the
McConnell household.

It was during the close of the war on 19th June, 1945, that
his mother died in child birth. James was seven years and eleven
months old and his sister Lila was fourteen.

His father, suffering from tuberculosis and cancer, was
hospitalised for some time, so it became clear that James would
need the aid of foster parents. The burning question he needed
answered was: who would take on the responsibility of raising
him? That duty fell to his grandparents, the Andersons.

He moved to their home in Perry Street in East Belfast,
and settled down to a new life.

Actually, his grandfather, Joseph Anderson, couldn't read
or write but when he accepted Christ as his Saviour he then
learned to read from the Bible. He was a man of prayer, a man
who believed in the words of James 5:16, "The effectual fervent
prayer of a righteous man availeth much."

He would regularly embarrass the rest of the family by boldly going into the next room and praying for them by name. He would even ask God to forgive their individual sins while they were still within earshot.

It was a small kitchen-type house where they lived. James slept in a single bed at the back of the house and always slept well. It was a peaceful home, and like Spring Street and the rest of the terraced houses in the area, it was without a garden. Around the walls hung Christian pictures, one in the hallway depicting a lamb, and the others mostly of Jesus, who was the only star in that house.

One of his favourite treats on coming home from school was getting a wee cup of tea, opening his grandfather's big Bible and reading from the book of Samuel. It was his favourite book in the Bible at that time.

Inevitably, the young James was strongly influenced by his grandfather who was an elder at the Iron Hall. James never missed a meeting there if at all possible.

James's grandmother, Margaret, was a good match for her husband Joseph in that she, too, was a staunch believer. Indeed, it was that spiritual guidance early in life which proved so important later on in the life of Joseph's young grandson.

As a child, James spent a considerable amount of time with his grandfather and this is how the bond between the two developed. It is unlikely that such a godly and discerning man as Joseph Anderson would not have been aware, even at that stage, that his grandson was chosen of God.

James would often be found in the house of God listening to his elders and asking them questions pertaining to spiritual matters. It was clear that his introduction to theology had already begun.

Apart from the Bible, the book that left the most lasting impression on Pastor McConnell was the story of William Carey, the cobbler sent to India.

It was the first book he ever read, and one that encouraged him greatly. He was influenced by Carey's dedication and the fact that Carey came from nothing. He too felt then that he had nothing to offer and couldn't see any real future for himself.

Inspired by this particular book, the young James learned all about the true meaning of character, something he would need in the days that lay ahead.

James warmly related to a story in the book where Carey climbed a tree, and fell off and broke his leg. When fully recovered from the accident, the first thing Carey did was to climb the tree again. Such a trait has become an ingrained part of James McConnell's personality over the years - a personality that has never given up easily on anything or anyone, particularly and significantly on those who have not yet received Christ as their own and personal Saviour.

Most of his time in those early days was spent reading God's Word. It seemed most appropriate that James devoted much of his youth to studying the Holy Bible, an essential beginning for any potential preacher, particularly one who would eventually attempt to reach a nation for God.

As a boy he would pray that God would make his mind like blotting paper, a mind able to soak up everything he read.

He would often go for a walk in the middle of the night and would preach to himself as he hurried along the streets of Belfast. One particular night he was walking and praying when suddenly he bumped into two people who were courting. To say they were surprised at hearing him pray was an understatement! That was the sort of thing that often happened to him.

With no parents to provide for him, young James was brought up poor, materially speaking, but never poor in spirit. He spent many hours totally content reading William Carey. He may have had no money and no real future at that point, but he is proof at least that, "godliness with contentment is great gain." I Tim 6:6.

That's not to say that he wasn't often insecure or apprehensive about his future, but God was about to give His servant a vision and a message that Jesus Christ was with him.

One evening, as he waited upon God, an old gas mantle became larger and larger, until it seemed the whole room was like a magnified and glorified light. This was no hallucination nor was it his imagination. Rather, like the prophecy given by the prophet Joel, it was the manifestation of the Holy Spirit.

He still recalls two verses from the book of Joel as being particularly significant. They are, "And it shall come to pass afterward, that I will pour out my spirit upon all flesh; and your sons and your daughters shall prophecy, your old men shall dream dreams, your young men shall see visions; and also upon the servants and upon the handmaids, in those days will I pour out my spirit." Joel 2:28,29.

The presence and power of that light was tremendous. The vision and message he received gave him the assurance that God was already at work in his life. From that night onward God poured out His Spirit upon him.

It wasn't the last time Almighty God visited James in such a dramatic way.

Chapter Three

ORPHANED, BUT NOT ALONE

❖

It was following his conversion that James had some tremendous experiences with God.

He began to talk to God in prayer in a wonderful way, which became a great help to him. His grandfather was often busy working down at the docks, while his grandmother, though very kind, was naturally not on his wave length.

So James formed the habit of meeting regularly with his Saviour and believes that all of those early circumstances were a divine part of God's purpose in developing him into the man he is today: a man who is watered daily by prayer, the most essential part of his life, not just now but also during his youth.

He tells how, throughout several boyhood years, he used to go into Belfast's Ormeau Park to play near the pond, before sneaking into the old part of the park to pray for many hours underneath the trees. That's not to say he didn't enjoy normal childhood interests. He loved nothing more than a game of soccer with his chums, but his conversion to Christ over-shadowed all of these things.

It was around the year 1950 when he first began to see the power of prayer. His sister Lila's health deteriorated to the extent that doctors gave her only a short time to live. Again a godly example was set by James's grandfather, who for a whole night lay prostrate on the floor of Belfast City Hospital asking God to spare his young granddaughter's life.

Certainly those prayers were answered in a most dramatic way as Lila recovered and, apart from a short spell in Whiteabbey hospital, went back to live at 14 Spring Street.

Sadly that same year, the young man witnessed the passing away of his dad, Edward McConnell. The former shipyard worker eventually died of cancer. Having earlier lost his mother, it was an event young James found hard to accept.

He felt so isolated. So alone. Like a ship without a rudder. He had no direction in life. Without parents, it was a most distressing time for a thirteen-year-old boy.

If ever a young man needed to have faith to cling to God's promises, it was young James. If there was any consolation for him at this time, it was the fact that both his parents had accepted Christ as their Saviour before they died. They had what is known as deathbed repentances. The fact that both of them went home to meet the Lord was of considerable comfort to James.

Despite the fact that he had little time to really get to know his dad before he died, James still remembers him with affection to this day.

James, however, was about to experience the providence and mighty power of the Holy Ghost in a way he would never forget. Orphaned he may have been, but alone he was not. For even at that embryonic stage God was with him, preparing him to preach the gospel and reach the lost at any price.

Following his father's funeral, he was walking along Belfast's Ravenhill Road towards his new school, Park Parade Secondary, when suddenly he began to call out to God. Tears of sadness rolled down his face, as he grieved for the parents he so desperately wanted to have.

Yet sadness was soon replaced by joy. Remarkably, he started to sing. For a brief moment he was entranced by the cross of Calvary. It was as if the Lord Jesus Christ was comforting him every step of the way.

Those early teenage years which followed were just as eventful. With an advanced prayer life for one so young and a deep understanding of God's Word, James was about to experience another poignant moment in his young life.

It was around this time that he began regularly attending the little hall on My Lady's Road, a Pentecostal building known as the Bible Pattern Church.

The elders thought so much of James, they allowed him to have the keys of the church. He was entrusted to open the doors early in the morning and to put on the heat. Those who knew James were intrigued as to how often he was drawn to God's house. Like his Master, James had learned to love the house of the Lord at an early age. For him, the best time for communion with God was early in the morning.

During one morning of such communion, he knelt down beside the heater and began to sing at the top of his voice just like his grandfather had taught him. Joseph Anderson used to sing below the stairs in his own house from an old Redemption hymn book and his young grandson was following that example. He too opened the old hymn book and began to sing:

"Take my life and let it be, consecrated Lord to thee."

James was asking God to take his life and use him for the glory of God.

Suddenly a woman, a complete stranger, burst into the room, walked up the aisle to where he sat and made him the focus of a God-inspired prophecy.

"You will preach the gospel to many nations and God will give you a mighty work which will reach out to other people. God is going to use you in a mighty way," she said.

James was stunned. He was certain that he had locked the doors. He was really quite scared.

Chapter Four

OPEN AIR TESTIMONY

❖

The Bible Pattern Church regularly held open-air gospel meetings each Sunday evening. One particular Lord's Day they arrived in Spring Street and parked right outside the home of James McConnell.

James was very concerned as many of his friends and football chums were always around. When the group arrived at his front door, it was his biggest test as a Christian up to that point. If he could have got away he would gladly have done so.

The next thing he knew, Head Constable Leeburn stood up and announced:

"You all know Jimmy McConnell. Well, he's going to tell you how the Lord saved him."

James wanted the ground to open up at this point. In fact he had been caught red-handed. But he steadied himself and for the very first time gave his public testimony, in his own street, outside his own front door.

It was a testimony heard by his friends, Jim Payne, Dougie Burns, Harry Thompson, Carlyle Bruce and John Boyd. His mates were surprised to hear James singing his head off.

When he was called upon to give his testimony, they all cheered and laughed, but he conducted himself in a loving manner and spoke with such conviction that they were soon silenced.

It was a daunting task that took courage in front of his mocking friends. He was known to his mates in those days as 'Sparky'. Indeed, before the event he concedes to having been a secret disciple and many of the people who knew him were taken by surprise when they heard his testimony.

Once he'd committed himself, though, there was no turning back.

"Jesus loves me," he shouted, so that everyone could hear. Another barrier had been broken. Another fence jumped.

James had always been someone special in the street. The thing most people remembered about him was how he loved to sing. He would be coming home from school and could be heard before he was seen.

Having now declared his intention to the entire street, he was instantly rewarded for taking his stand. Indeed his public testimony was significant in that it was also the birth of James McConnell, the preacher.

As soon as he gave his testimony that night, he knew for the first time that he was called to preach. Oh, how he wanted to do that. It was a burning, insatiable desire.

The feelings were indeed similar to his boyhood hero C. H. Spurgeon, who, after realising that he too was called to preach, later penned the words:

"How I loved my Saviour Christ then! I would have given all I had for Him! How I felt towards sinners that day! Lad that I was, I wanted to preach and say to sinners around, what a dear Saviour I had found."

In the case of James McConnell, all of those wonderful experiences as a boy with the Lord suddenly hit home. He could see for the first time why he felt different from other boys his age. He recognised instantly that what he had inside was clearly a definite calling - despite his tender years.

The evening proved to be a major turning point in his life. From that night, his friends, his football, everything was forgotten. The world just totally disappeared.

Chapter Five

FIRST SERMONS

❖

It was still well before the 'troubles'. The street lamps may have been a lot dimmer than they are today, but at least men, women and children could walk home safely after dark.

One of those youngsters was James McConnell. He was used to walking home in the dark, although he was afraid of the entry near his house. In fact, he armed himself with a brick in one hand, and a stick in the other.

One particular night, during his early teens, he was walking along Mount Street, near Belfast's Woodstock Road, when he heard a group of people praying. It was well past his bedtime, but unlike other boys his age who would probably have walked on, he stopped and listened outside the house.

The words he heard were these, "Lord, we are seeking you and we are not sure if this baptism in the Holy Ghost is for tonight. We are frightened of tongues and the manifestations that accompany this experience, yet we feel there is something in it and we need this confirmed."

Quick as a flash, young James knocked at the window of the house and disturbed the meeting. Allowed to come inside, he proceeded to address the room full of adult believers, "For the promise is unto you and to your children and to them that are afar off, even as many as the Lord our God shall call, Acts 2:38. That's your answer," he boldly declared.

Shock and bewilderment was in that room. Mouths fell open at the sight of this young whippersnapper who had dared to be different, courageously confirming God's word for them.

If ever a group of people were privileged to witness the anointing of God upon a young man's life, it was that group of believers who had gathered to pray in Mount Street.

It was the quickest answer to prayer those people ever got in their lives. They were overwhelmed, but still able to offer James a cup of tea.

Inevitably, preaching engagements followed, such as the opportunity to preach his first sermon. The Bible Pattern Church had such a high regard for James they asked him to speak following the breaking of bread at one of their Lord's Day services. He arrived with one sheet of paper, a little Bible and a text from Psalm 22 entitled, "My God, My God, why hast thou forsaken me."

Given the events of his childhood, perhaps the title of the sermon was most appropriate, yet the comprehensive nature and overall content of the Word was nevertheless quite detailed for one so young.

Experienced ministers with unquestionable maturity might have had difficulty preaching such a message, yet here was a fourteen-year-old boy speaking competently on the subject in front of a full congregation. Although he has preached the sermon many times since, James still believes the first time was better than any other.

He was inspired by the many great preachers in Ulster forty years ago. There were some tremendous orators then and young James loved to hear them. People like Frank Knox and Willie Mullan thrilled his soul.

Another man who inspired James McConnell to a life of preaching was George Jeffreys, particularly after James paid a visit to the Wellington Hall to listen to him. Jeffreys was approaching the twilight of his career, but nevertheless the young boy remained in awe of him.

Jeffreys mounted the pulpit wearing a black blazer and striped trousers, with a black and white spotted tie. His text taken from Acts chapter four was entitled, "Lord behold their threatenings." But it was afterwards that he really left an impression with James. As the young boy was putting on his coat, George Jeffreys put his arms around him and asked:

"What are you doing, my boy?"

"Please, sir, I'm getting my coat," replied James.

At that point Jeffreys put the youngster's coat on for him and encouraged him with the announcement, "God's hand is upon you, boy."

That had a profound effect on his life. He skipped home in the rain, delighted that God had used such a great man to speak to a little boy like him.

Over the next few years, James found great stability in the Bible Pattern Church. He was in fact spoiled by the members, who, aware that he was an orphan boy, took a considerable interest in him.

Yet they were equally aware of something else. These simple, kind and humble people also sensed that God's hand was upon the boy's life even at that stage, particularly following his debut sermon.

Two of these people, Billy and Lily Towell, were particularly helpful to James. Billy was impressed by him from the day he got saved. James was back and forward to Billy's house singing:

"My heart is fixed, eternal God, fixed on thee,

And my immortal choice is made, Christ for me."

James sensed the dawning of a new era. He knew that he had been called to preach and what's more, he relished the thought of doing just that.

Chapter Six

LED BY A STRANGER

❖

Following his first sermon, various people heard about the precocious young preacher, who was then flooded with invitations to preach at other halls.

As his experience developed through preaching, especially at open-air meetings, it became obvious that this was indeed his gift.

But it was the open-air work that mainly inspired him. He used to seek the Lord and, after he had been given his orders by the Holy Spirit, he would go and stand in the middle of a certain street and preach. Some people thought that the young man was crazy.

As God quickened him and educated him for future years, the youngster's capacity for prayer and reading of God's Word began to increase, to the extent that he believed God was about to call him to a very specific task.

He was now 15 years old and readily engaged in study for the ministry, even though he had left school, and, like his late father, was now employed in Belfast's Harland and Wolff shipyard as an office boy.

Lots of Ulster people worked at the shipyard which at that time was easily Northern Ireland's largest work-force. Over 20,000 people were employed at Belfast docks.

During this time a man called Bob Martin, head of the design squad, took a liking to James and significantly brought great comfort to him at a most crucial stage. He was James's supervisor, an unsaved man, but he showed James great kindness after finding out that he was an orphan boy. In fact, after he had informed the other men of his circumstances, they totally spoiled him. These six men showed James unrivalled consideration.

It was yet another indication of how God was bringing people as helpers into the young boy's life. These men took James under their wing in every department. They schooled him in how to do his job, and even visited his sister in hospital, giving her money each weekend.

It now seemed quite natural for the Lord to call James for a specific purpose, but he had a few lessons to learn before he began to preach in earnest, namely, that if you disobey the Holy Spirit, God will let you know and if you are a praying man or woman you will be the first to know.

In one particular case, James was about to experience an emptiness in his spiritual life like never before. During a morning prayer session, he recalls being told by the Holy Spirit to visit another group of believers in Belfast who were not exactly popular. Instead of going straight there, he was stubborn and hesitant, even sharing his commission with older Christians, themselves alarmed at where he was to go.

One elderly lady who had a dream claimed she saw him drowning in a river, with no friends on hand to help.

"Don't go," she said, and, ill advised, he didn't.

But there was a price to pay for not doing as the Spirit had commanded. The weeks that followed were lonely. For the first time, he wasn't touching God the way he used to. Moreover, God wasn't touching him like He used to. Gone was that sharpness. Instead he became sluggish and slow and even more concerning was the fact that he was struggling to pray.

Eventually such apathy spilled over to his place of work. He was oversleeping and arriving late at the shipyard. No longer was he punching the clock one hour early. There were no more prayer times during his walk to work. Worship was replaced by worry and a showdown with his Saviour inevitably arrived.

Things came to a head when James arrived for work one morning. Although frightened of lifts, he stopped it midway and cried out, "Father, what have I done?"

"You have done nothing," came a still small voice and suddenly he knew what the Spirit was telling him to do.

But he had reservations. "Nobody likes these people, they are heretics," he protested.

"Go!" the Spirit persisted.

Finally James decided to obey.

This time he was not to be deterred and when the lift reached its destination, he walked out to be greeted by curious stares.

James was now back in the centre of God's will, having gone, as the Lord commanded, to that unpopular church.

It was November 5th, 1953, and he remembers going into work early one morning through wind and rain and glad to get to his desk. Just as he sat down a man approached him and said:

"Thus saith the Lord, I want to show you something. I want to show you a warehouse. In this warehouse there are all kinds of great vessels; there's a man in this warehouse and he's filling these vessels with oil. Some are large, others medium and small, but all of the vessels are filled to capacity with oil.

You are one of these vessels and the man with the oil- can is the Lord. It is up to you to determine how large a vessel you will become for God. You can become a large, medium or small vessel, but if you give yourself to the Lord, dedicate yourself and increase that dedication, then He will fill you more and more."

The man then said, "Good morning," and left.

It was a message that left him speechless, one that shook him greatly. How could he ever again doubt that God was in his life in the power of the Holy Spirit? Once he had pulled himself together, he followed the man to the front door, but it was too late. He had disappeared.

Day after day at dinner break, the young boy began to look for a place to seek the Lord, but for some time couldn't find it. He would often walk down the road singing and praying out loud, while back at the office other men were tucking into fish and chips or a packed lunch. Like Job, who esteemed the words of God's mouth more than his necessary food, Job 23:12, it was more important for James to be found in the presence of the Lord than to eat with his workmates.

Finding a quiet place proved almost impossible, until one day James stumbled across an old broken-down bus. An ideal place to worship and pray in private.

As he did so, other believers in the shipyard, much older than himself, were intrigued, eventually asking to join him. One brother soon became two until there was a bus full of these young men all of whom, with the exception of one, are involved in the ministry today.

Due to that message on a November morning, allied to the increased effort to find the will of God in his life, another chapter in the life of James McConnell was about to unfold.

Indeed God was about to bring two important men into his life - Pastors James Forsythe and Gordon Magee - men who many believers looked upon as being controversial and heretical, due to their association with the Church of God in Ulster. It was seen as a contentious assembly for its doctrinal emphasis. But James refutes to this day claims that Pastors Forsythe and Magee were heretics.

He was an orphan and they made their homes available to him for love, comfort and teaching. These two pastors had the ability and foresight to see the grace of God in his life and they gave him essential encouragement to pursue his ministry. He found these men to be godly men of zeal and men with big hearts. Above all, though, men who were in love with Jesus Christ.

These Pastors were clearly sent to shape the young man's future, for in the years that followed James Forsythe taught James junior how to worship and pray, while Gordon Magee who was a master in the art of preaching, taught the young servant how to put across the message of God's grace for sinners and to prepare such a sermon.

It was during those formative years that both men had a real and lasting impact upon the life of the young boy.

Their early encouragement and tuition would eventually help James to accomplish the work a hundredfold.

Just like the stranger in the shipyard had planned it.

Chapter Seven

A BOY PREACHER

❖

During the mid-nineteen fifties, James had a desire to join the Church of God at Devon Parade.

Shortly after he was received into fellowship he was asked by Pastor James Forsythe to preach at a youth rally. It was a memorable night for the young Spring Street boy whose subject was, "The Church of the Laodiceans."

As the weeks progressed he made rapid advances in the Christian life. He developed spiritually well beyond his years and from that night at the youth rally he never stopped preaching.

By now, he was preaching the gospel approximately three times a week. Souls were being saved and invitations arrived from England to speak at other youth missions and conventions.

Soon, the Lord's work began to interfere with his employment at the shipyard. He was totally immersed in praying, studying and witnessing. It had become obvious that his days at Harland and Wolff were numbered.

Significantly, though, his sermons impressed many of his older brethren, who believed they had in their midst a very special young man.

For example, after a group of ministers from many parts of the world laid hands on him, ordaining him to become an evangelist, no fewer than five hundred people came to Christ in that same year under his ministry. He was just eighteen years of age. During his youth, he had shown God his heart of trust and now it appeared God was repaying that trust by giving him an early anointing to win souls.

It was reward for a character formed by daily discipline and daily duties, such as his prayer times, daily readings and even visitations. He was working out his own salvation, but not without strength, help and conversation with Christ.

Though amazed, even nervous, about the opportunities God was providing during this time, the pastor was greatly attracted by the challenge. He was very nervous because at that particular time the Devon Parade Church was full of young men who were great preachers and he was very conscious of preaching in front of them, but the Lord blessed him.

Once he had got up to speak, the boy preacher found it hard to stop. He was motivated by a desire to serve the Lord and the thrill as a boy of getting up to speak in front of packed halls.

More advanced than many older ministers, he became, as James Spurgeon expressed it about his brother Charles, "A marvellous example of a preacher leaping at a bound, full grown in the pulpit."

It was not James's privilege, however, to go to Bible School and he even wondered if he would have been accepted at that particular time. He didn't feel he had the education to go and, since his family had no money, he wasn't encouraged to attend, either.

He didn't feel worthy of such an opportunity. Moreover, he used to ask himself the question, "How could a young man from such an unpretentious background be considered for Bible School?"

But he was to learn throughout his life the significance of what Paul spoke of in I Corinthians 1:26-29, "For ye see your calling, brethren, how that not many wise men after the flesh, not many mighty, not many noble, are called: But God hath chosen the foolish things of the world to confound the wise; and God hath chosen the weak things of the world to confound the mighty; And base things of the world, and things which are despised, hath God chosen, yea, and things which are not, to bring to nought things that are: That no flesh should glory in his presence."

Certainly God had chosen both Gordon Magee and James Forsythe to look after the young man. Actually, it was at this point of his ministry that they became a vital influence.

He spent many years living with and watching these two godly men at work. They educated him and trained him and in that sense he didn't need a Bible School. They were his spiritual teachers.

The young preacher was often asked to return to many churches during his youth, but he had to turn those same invitations down. There was one offer, however, that he just couldn't refuse.

After successfully leading the Easter Conventions in Ulster he was certain that God had called him into the ministry. Knowing also that the land of England stood in great need of the gospel, he agreed to do 'pulpit supply' for a minister in the North of England. It proved to be the end of his time in the shipyard.

It was an Easter Monday night when ministers laid hands on him and repeated the earlier prophecy which stated that he would preach to many nations throughout the world. For a while he went to Belfast's Shankill Road, where he preached every Sunday, but then came his first opportunity.

The English minister of Gateshead had to visit the USA and told young James if he stood in for him he would receive a good salary. James went, not for the money, but for the opportunity to preach the gospel.

When, however, he landed in Newcastle-upon-Tyne carrying two cases, he wept with loneliness, despite the new challenge in his life.

It was now 1955 and the woman he was staying with was a widow, and not exactly well off. Some days were so tough they both had to gather lemonade bottles and brought them to the shops in return for food. It was a test of his faith and dedication to the Lord Jesus Christ.

Nevertheless, it wasn't long before he was addressing large crowds who flocked to hear him. What had started out as a few soon grew into a multitude.

People came not only from Gateshead, but from the surrounding north-east countryside. The building was packed to capacity as James began to influence the congregation. He displayed a gift for which he was to become renowned throughout his later ministry, the gift of challenging the souls of men, both in and out of the pulpit.

During a prolific four-month period, he talked to all sorts: Geordie coalminers, alcoholics and prostitutes, many of whom gave their lives to the Lord Jesus Christ. He knew these people and their families by name. He recognised sin which was everywhere, he prayed for the sick, comforted the suffering and witnessed to people from all backgrounds until the entire area was literally transformed.

One night in particular stands out. It was October 1955, and he had been out walking the roads of Gateshead and Newcastle praying and crying unto God that He might manifest His power and presence to him in a powerful way. To say he received an answer to those prayers can still be described as an understatement.

It was a Sunday night just prior to the service. He and his colleagues were having a time of prayer after which James was the last to leave the vestry. As he closed the door behind him, he noticed the front row was full of visitors, whom he understood to be from other local congregations. As he climbed the steps to the pulpit a beautifully dressed lady and her daughter fell on their faces.

The pastor was alarmed, as he had always been used to order and respect in his meetings. He rushed down to the front row to enquire what had happened.

"Vicar, did you see him?" the onlookers enquired breathlessly.

"See who?" asked James, bewildered.

"The figure with a long, white coat walking up the steps before you," came the startling reply.

Overwhelmed, he proceeded with the opening hymn, but many of the congregation just stared as the light was apparently still there. People fell to the floor and one woman shouted, "Jesus is in this place, He's in you."

Even before the young pastor preached many people cried for mercy that night and were healed. The atmosphere was electrifying.

When he first arrived in England he was introduced to a congregation of thirty people, but by Christmas over five to six hundred worshippers were attending on a regular basis.

Then he returned home to Belfast shortly afterwards to take a mission in Devon Parade. During a ten-day period, over 35 people were saved and baptised, It was a remarkable mission, as all of those converts went on with God. One of those saved was his sister Lila, who gave her life to Christ during those days. This was a tremendous thrill for James.

Meanwhile the original pastor of Gateshead returned to his office and when nobody showed up, he asked:

"Where is this so-called revival?"

The saintly lady who had looked after James, replied, "The revival went, Sir, when the young man went home."

It marked the end of that particular man's pastorate at Gateshead and before long the church members pleaded with James to return until such times as they got a regular pastor. Return he did for three months and yet again five to seven hundred worshippers came flooding back to hear him.

Although he was developing spiritually at this time, he still had much to learn about the everyday ministry. But it was during those teenage years in England that James displayed much of the character that later radiated from him so prominently.

Indeed, what astounded his English congregation was the reality and earnestness of his public ministry and the sheer power of his preaching for one so young, not to mention the obvious control of his messages.

Inevitably after his three-month stay in Gateshead he felt led to come back to Belfast for what he thought would be a short time. Instead God had drawn his ministry in Newcastle to an end, a parting he found hard to accept.

By now, however, many of his English-based flock had already resigned themselves to losing their young preacher. Naturally their prayers were with him, but they were left despondent by his untimely removal. He had made close friends with many of his congregation in Newcastle, and it seemed such a shame to have to move on. The Lord had other ideas for his servant, however. Another flock was waiting for him in Belfast, even though he was totally unaware of this.

As Theodore Epp wrote in his book, 'God Planned It For Good': "God is not an opportunist. He does not wait until the circumstances are right to take action. Rather, God in His sovereignty brings about the circumstances which produce the right time for Him to act."

God had been carefully watching over and training James for the task he had chosen him and caused him to dream about. Now, after years of waiting amid great trials and many temptations, His man was about to see why God had worked in such ways in his life.

A return to his roots, the province of Ulster, paved the way for an historic beginning.

Something bigger, greater, grander, was about to unfold.

Chapter Eight

I'M THE MAN

❖

Having returned from England, he was now living at Onslow Gardens, in Belfast, at the home of Pastor James Forsythe. His other spiritual mentor, Pastor Gordon Magee, lived directly opposite the house, which made it easy for both men to keep in touch, especially when helping and encouraging young James.

As the boy preacher developed further still, offers to speak all over Europe began to surface. Trips to Holland, Germany, Denmark and Sweden were provisionally pencilled in, as was a tour of the United States of America. The world was his oyster and all before his 20th birthday.

Here was a magnificent platform to make himself a famed evangelist, something he had always dreamed of becoming. Beneath the quiet surface of a committed Christian preacher, however, one strong tide was flowing - Holy ambition.

The fact that the earlier prophecy was still ringing in his ears, namely, that the Lord would send him to many nations to preach the gospel, left him drawing only one conclusion. He was irrevocably convinced that God, not man, had opened these doors to progress and so became extremely excited.

What's more, he was being offered large sums of money to take up these appointments and was being sent gifts from many different and well-meaning sources. Several other preachers he knew of had gone abroad and were sending back encouraging reports.

It was a tremendous prospect and he was enjoying life at that time.

It was clear also to both Pastors James Forsythe and Gordon Magee that James McConnell was a gifted young preacher. But he was about to understand the words of the prophet Isaiah, who, under the influence of the Holy Spirit, said, "For my thoughts are not your thoughts, neither are your ways my ways, saith the Lord." Isaiah 55:8.

This zealous, enthusiastic preacher was not about to hit the bright lights or experience instant fame and fortune at all. God had other plans for him. On the contrary, he was about to face severe poverty and be brought back to earth with a bump.

In fact he was to experience 12 years of loneliness, with no money and what appeared to be no future. James would become buried in a pioneering work in a little Orange Hall on the Whitewell Road.

But not before the leading of the Lord first.

One afternoon, while still captivated at the prospect of international travel, he was preparing a sermon when in walked James Forsythe and Gordon Magee. To James's surprise, Pastor Magee said, "There are at least 10 people living in the Greencastle area who would like to start a church. We are inviting you to take it on."

Shocked, even disappointed, the young man replied, "Look at all these other engagements I have. It would be impossible. I'm sorry, but I think I'll have to pass on this one."

Both James Forsythe and Gordon Magee accepted his decision, but made it clear that he was the man to whom they wanted to give the first option. James looked at their faces and knew they were disappointed, but he stuck to his decision, nevertheless.

For the next few days, James couldn't eat, drink or sleep and became extremely troubled in his spirit. He wasn't burdened about the pastors' proposal only. It was far worse than that. He was literally and physically disturbed.

As letters poured in confirming his visits to various countries, he couldn't get excited about them any more. He knew something wasn't quite right, especially as his prayer life had broken down. As had happened on other occasions in his life, when he either deliberately or unintentionally walked out of God's will, he was struggling to pray and touch God in the normal way.

Then the Holy Spirit spoke to him, saying:

"What are you going to do about these 10 people?"

It was the most important question he had ever been asked. One that left him completely speechless.

Meanwhile, it became a complex matter as he was about to find out, for while he deliberated over whether to accept the appointment, another man had been interviewed by the two men and had gladly agreed to start the work.

When young James heard about it, he announced defiantly, "He's not the man - I'm the man."

This left Pastor Gordon Magee in a most difficult position, and he was not amused. Panic-stricken, the boy continued:

"I say this with respect, if you send that man down there, he will achieve nothing whatsoever."

It was at this point he reiterated that the Holy Ghost had told him he must take up the appointment.

He was actually in the house, washing dishes, when God spoke to him and said, "You must take this opportunity, you must take it."

James embraced the opportunity forcibly and it proved to be the beginning of his life's work. A great and effectual door had been opened. Little did he know that he had sentenced himself to servitude, where he would be scraping and scrounging to make ends meet.

The Whitewell calling was a traumatic experience for him. He felt he was taking a backward step in his career. You may ask, why then did he accept such an invitation? The conviction was powerful. It was like a sinner getting right with God. He knew in his heart that if he had decided on a career elsewhere, he might never have found the centre of God's will for his life.

Convinced by his sincerity, both pastors went back to the other man, made their apologies and then appointed James. God had given His servant a second chance.

Like David looking after a few sheep, following the ewes with young, listening to them, loving them, caring for them and practically carrying them, James had been called to be a good shepherd at Greencastle, a place far removed from the dizzy heights he had in mind for himself.

It was now October 1956, and for the remainder of that year he would be found doing what he has become renowned for over the years, knocking at doors and asking people to come and hear him preach.

Rising early in the morning, his day was packed with studying, visiting, praying, but mostly preparing his heart for his new challenge. By now, he had given up his favourite sport, soccer, and had no personal friendships. All his time and energy were given to the Lord.

Having not entered a college environment, where he may have had to conform to the same level as ordinary individuals, he was not restricted in his faith. Indeed without the usual mouldings of men, he was not carrying any baggage and was tremendously excited at the prospect of preaching in his very own pulpit.

Naturally, however, he was filled with some apprehension. In that little room of his at Onslow Gardens, he still longed for his flock in Gateshead, England, almost petrified at the thought of his new challenge. There was safety in numbers there, but in Belfast he was starting from scratch.

In fact he was about to begin a fellowship with just ten people in an old building at the bottom of the Whitewell Road, Belfast. Not exactly the ideal setting for a church.

The child of God had grown and for the first time he was being asked to leave his nest of comfortability in exchange for the uncertain and more precarious life of the unknown. Even though God had his best interests at heart, James still felt terribly isolated.

But God knew that the thrill of ministerial soaring could only begin with the fear of falling and, like the mother eagle, Almighty God also knew that until his chosen child discovered true Christian wings, there would be no purpose to his life - hence the push out of that nest was the greatest gift He had to offer.

To James, it may have seemed like a backward step, but to God it was a giant leap forward down the Christian road.

Like the Bible says, "As an eagle stirreth up her nest, fluttereth over her young, spreadeth abroad her wings, taketh them, beareth them on her wings. So the Lord did lead him ... and there was no strange god with him." Deut. 32:11, 12.

PART TWO

WAXED STRONG IN SPIRIT

Chapter Nine

The First Years at Whitewell

HUMBLE BEGINNINGS

---------------- ❖ ----------------

I t wasn't quite the stable of Bethlehem, but the humble beginnings of the Metropolitan Church, Belfast, were no less obscure.

That first morning it was snowing. The old Orange Hall which was rented was reeking with beer smells from the night before and a young man, together with a fellow worker, brushed up the cigarette ends and opened the windows to let in some fresh air.

At just 19 years old, the orphan boy from Spring Street, East Belfast, was clearing the debris in time for his opening services.

It began with 10 people, plus 12 visitors, making a grand total of 22. One man recollecting the occasion spoke with a smile as he recalled the young skinny preacher announcing in revolutionary language about a great work that was going to start in the Greencastle area.

"You will remember this day," he said, "It is the beginning of months of tears, hardships and difficulties - but if you are faithful, God will breathe upon us by His Spirit and give us a people that will touch this land.

This church will become a reaping church and will benefit the community. God will bring into our midst hundreds of young people and many visitors will come to us from around the world to witness what the Lord has accomplished among us."

In the late fifties, though, such an accomplishment seemed a long way off. Immediately after the prophecy, James moved from his home in East Belfast to be with his new flock in the north of the city.

At first he lived in a small flat, but eventually in the early part of 1958 James purchased his own home in the district of Newtownabbey. He settled at Doagh Road for about three years in a little terraced house, only moving on when he met and married his wife Margaret.

Yet despite the modest beginnings of his home and church, nothing could detract from the excitement of preaching that first morning to his new assembly. The Orange Hall was mostly of wooden construction and not very attractive.

The area then was mainly Protestant, with many from a working class background. If there was a plus factor to the pastor's early ministry, it was simply that he didn't have a hard act to follow. His church had no history. For him it was a case of sink or swim.

All James could see as he entered the pulpit that first Sunday was the challenge that lay before him.

Feelings of insecurity departed as he concentrated on the preaching of the gospel of Jesus Christ. After all, it was to be his vocation for the rest of his life and he was determined to start well.

It seems so appropriate now that the subject and title of his evening sermon was, "The obedience of faith." It was a text taken from Hebrews chapter 11. He expanded on how, "by faith Abraham, was called to go out into a place which he should after receive for an inheritance, obeyed." The congregation began to marvel at the young preacher's great depth of understanding of his subject.

At the evening service, numbers had swelled to around 60 as, during the afternoon, news of this activity spread like wildfire to the surrounding area. The Orange Hall was normally used for other purposes, for example, band practices.

Yet that night there wasn't a single drum beating. Instead the hall was almost filled to capacity as people thronged to hear the preaching of the gospel: but not without some form of criticism. Similar to events during the life of Christ, modern-day scribes and pharisees were never far away and many persons had gathered to cast the first stone in great disapproval. Like Spurgeon, who was called a heretic because he was not a college graduate, James, too, was labelled a charlatan, because he wasn't ordained at that time.

But the conviction of his preaching soon gave evidence of his love for his congregation. As he ministered, it became apparent that he wasn't showing off and his new members sensed it. The facts were that his training in England had made him robust, despite his tender years. He was like a breath of fresh air for the people of the area, who, in time, were impressed by his single-minded devotion to the cause of Christ and the conversion of sinners that resulted from his preaching.

He made no distinction between Protestant, Catholic, Jew or agnostic. He saw them as precious souls in need of a Saviour. Indeed his people soon asked, with growing interest, "Who is this young man?"

Alongside him were established assemblies such as Methodist, Presbyterian, Church of Ireland and Brethren. Yet here was a raw 19-year-old recruit starting another work for God on a wing and a prayer, in the very same community.

Such courage brought instant reward. The people were delighted with their new man and went out of their way to encourage others to attend, in case the pastor packed up and left prematurely. Nothing could have been further from the truth, however. James had no intention of being a one-sermon wonder.

He regularly read the Saturday night edition of the Belfast Telegraph which advertised Pastor Willie Mullan's Bible Class in Lurgan. At the time Pastor Mullan was speaking to approximately 600 people, while James had just 30-40 souls.

He admits going to Lurgan a couple of nights just to absorb the atmosphere, but he always felt uncomfortable in case his own people needed him.

As Eliab said to David, "With whom hast thou left those few sheep in the wilderness?" I Sam. 17 v. 28. so the young Belfast shepherd was concerned about his own pasture.

Individuals were, and still are, very important to him.

Chapter Ten

A MAN OF PRAYER

❖

I f his church had a strength over the years, it has most
certainly been in the willingness of the members to pray.
It was surely this one single quality that helped the church
at Whitewell wax strong in spirit and it was a quality taught by
the young pastor himself.

From his earliest days in Spring Street, James has been a
prayer warrior. Such was his zeal and belief in the power of
prayer, he would open his own home to his congregation when
the Orange Hall was not available. He always expected to see
God answer prayer both in his own life and in the life of his
members.

Every night for two years prayer meetings were held.
People were encouraged to pray and pray they did. Yet the
prayer life of the pastor was the greatest motivation to them.
No formal requests or false performances. Just a man who loved
Jesus and told Him so in simple terms.

There were no grand introductions or theological tours of
the scriptures in the pastor's own public prayers. He got straight

to the point and asked God to meet the needs of his people who, he says, have become his family. It's almost as if his praying was superior to his gift of preaching. As William Williams said of Spurgeon, "When bowed before God in family prayer, he appeared a grander man even than when holding thousands of people spellbound by his oratory."

James exhorted his members to come to God with confidence. "Leave every request with Jesus; He has everything in control," he would insist.

The result was astonishing. God heard those prayers and answered many of them. Friends and family members were reached by God and saved for time and eternity. People who were suffering from severe illnesses were healed. Notably, however, others in the Whitewell area heard about the church and began to attend.

They were inspired after hearing that the people of Whitewell and their pastor were locked inside that building night after night, crying unto the Lord for mercy. "What sort of people pray every single night without a break?" many of those curious onlookers enquired.

People who had faith and people who had a great desire to see their God move on their behalf, was the answer.

It wasn't always serious. There were many nights when the Holy Spirit introduced a bit of humour.

The pastor could never forget those faithful prayer warriors: men and women filled with a vision. People who believed that God would use their pastor in a wonderful way. James was not just their pastor, he was their friend. They had empathy and passion for his own desire to build a great church in the area and his flock agreed with him that unless many hours of prayer and supplication were invested, then circumstances would not change.

James recalls one lady by the name of Nellie Garrett, who joined the church at Whitewell in 1958. She went on to become one of his true partners in prayer as did a lady by the name of Lizzie McDonald. Known affectionately as 'Mum,' the pastor remembers Lizzie as one of the most solid and faithful members he has ever had. 'Mum' was with him until the early nineties and was an example of godliness and love.

She, like hundreds of his flock over the years, had a mind to pray and work for her Saviour.

As James McConnell began his ministry, he did so in the knowledge and confidence that his own people were bearing him up in the place of prayer. Not just praying, though, but crying unto God on behalf of themselves, their church and their pastor.

There can be no greater compliment, no greater sacrifice from a congregation, than that.

Chapter Eleven

BEHIND EVERY GOOD MAN

---- ❖ ----

Despite being totally immersed in God's work, James was nevertheless keen to find himself a spiritual companion.

Unknown to him at that time a girl called Margaret Foster was intrigued not so much by his personality but by his fervent style of preaching.

She first laid eyes on James when he was ministering as a young preacher at Belfast's Church of God, Devon Parade. Margaret was going to the Church of God because she had suffered illness and needed healing. There was a man who prayed for the sick at the East Belfast church and so she went along to receive a blessing.

James, however, was actively involved in Devon Parade at the time, but more as a song leader. When he did take to the pulpit, though, Margaret was most impressed.

She thought he was great - a remarkable preacher for his age and a man who had obviously great potential. Mind you, he didn't really attract her as a person then , even though she visited his house quite a bit to meet with his sister Lila. Once she got to know him Margaret could see other qualities and it was then that she began to have romantic feelings towards him.

Those feelings, however, were not quickly reciprocated. She wondered if there was any romance in James at all. The first time he showed any signs was when he called at her house and, out of the blue, asked Margaret to go out with him. She accepted.

It was the start of what has been a life-long friendship, though in Margaret's case those early days of courtship meant great sacrifice. She couldn't really put a time on anything as James was always preaching. It was very difficult to continue a normal relationship with someone like that and Margaret admits that, at one point, they nearly split up.

The day of reckoning came after they were engaged and, fed up with hanging around, the young lady decided to return the engagement ring. James, however, got into an awful panic, so she held on to it.

It was a decision Margaret has never regretted. She became hugely influenced by James spiritually; in her own words, "I came out of my shell as I was a bit reserved and not very knowledgable regarding God's Word."

The main obstacle to her faith at the time was lack of spiritual teaching, but with the help of the Devon Parade church, particularly the preaching of her husband-to-be, she was never left hungry for fresh bread again. Margaret had accepted Christ as her Saviour but hadn't grown in her faith during this period. But as the weeks and months went by, James began to lead her along the paths of righteousness. She gradually experienced a true relationship with the Lord Jesus Christ and had a much better understanding of the message of the cross.

They began to meet regularly, going for walks in Victoria Park and along the Newtownards Road. But most of their time was spent attending meetings at Devon Parade Church, something they both enjoyed and were committed to, which in itself was a sign of great compatibility.

As the relationship blossomed, their hearts became joined, especially at their engagement party, which also marked James's

21st birthday. This event took place at Pastor James Forsythe's house.

Many of the pastors in the area attended, along with James and Margaret's closest friends and family. It was a lovely day and one that stands out for Margaret much more than any other.

The pair were engaged for about a year before they were married on April Fool's Day, 1959, at Devon Parade Church. Pastor James Forsythe conducted the ceremony. They stopped off at Whiteabbey, before leaving for a little church in the country where James was preaching.

Almost forty years later Margaret is still waiting for a honeymoon. But she doesn't think she will get it as James's desire for God's work and commitment to his flock is the same as it ever was.

The absence of a honeymoon was not solely due to James being very busy. He had just started in Whitewell and with a congregation of twenty or thirty people, simply hadn't the money.

Some nights James would return to their home at King's Park, Whiteabbey, utterly exhausted after ministering to his flock. Despite being a rugged and fearless young preacher, James also has a soft side to his character and at the end of a strenuous day his loving wife was just the sort of companion he needed.

He walked four or six times daily to Whitewell in those days, which kept him out of the house for long periods. As the ministry grew, he would be away even longer, preaching in places like Holland and Germany. It was a lonely time for the pastor's wife, being married for such a short period.

What she struggled with most was the amount of time her husband was spending with other people. Actually, over the years that zeal that he had for his flock made her a little angry on occasions, but in her own words, "I have usually caught myself on."

Margaret's feelings of resentment were not directed towards the Lord, however. In her case, she became used to her husband spending more and more time with God. Many times he would slip on his coat and leave to seek the face of God, either by car or by foot, but she learned to accept it.

There was some consolation for Margaret during all those lonely hours ... the birth of their first child, Linda, on 1st January, 1961. It would be six more years before their second daughter Julie arrived on 12th July, 1967.

At that particular time, the Whitewell people knew little of what can best be described as 'supernatural experiences'. They would have to wait a few more years to see the realisation of the Holy Spirit in their lives in this respect.

Supernatural experiences, although not discussed outside the McConnell household, were commonplace inside it.

For example, after the couple were first married, Margaret noticed that when James was in his study, he would be talking with another person. Since no one came into the house she naturally wondered what was going on. She couldn't hear the other person's voice, but from the conversations which took place she knew James wasn't praying. This didn't happen on just one occasion, but many. There were times when she could hear him shouting at what was obviously the enemy. "Clear off and leave me alone," he would scream, while at other times he would speak to God in a very personal way.

Having said this, Margaret has always been most discreet, even with her husband, about such incidents. She didn't make a habit of listening at the door as she quickly realised that the messenger of the Lord was guiding her partner on a regular basis.

"It wouldn't have been right to do that, as a person's relationship with the Lord is private," says Margaret.

Here is touching evidence of supreme love and respect for her husband. Other spouses may have considered it their right to listen during those wonderful encounters James had with the Holy Spirit, but his faithful wife was not of such a disposition.

Yet Margaret wasn't the only person in the McConnell household to notice strange happenings in her husband's study and bedroom. Their daughter Julie was just a child when she heard her dad having loud conversations in his bedroom. She remembers hearing him talking to someone, even though she knew there was no-one else in the room. She thought he was losing his reason and ran downstairs and said, "Mummy, there is somebody in the room with Daddy." Margaret then went upstairs with Julie, who was only about eight years old, but when she heard the familiar language being used she took her daughter aside and explained, "Daddy is just praying."

As Julie grew older, those incidents became more frequent. Even when her dad walked around the house he would be talking to himself and if he was in the bath he would splash around shouting out loud. He was practising his preaching and praying to God.

Despite those lonely years, Margaret's allegiance to her husband has never wavered. She has been a truly ideal partner for James. Indeed she contends that they are, and always have been, close companions.

Here again was God's divine providence. Having had such an uncertain childhood, security at home was important for this servant of God. He needed a loving and loyal wife, who believed in him and prayed for him in all that he undertook to accomplish for God. To marry a selfish wife, who needed to be seen and heard, would have been disastrous.

Margaret's unselfish life and commitment to her husband has more than proven true the old saying ... "behind every good man, there's an even better woman."

Chapter Twelve

THE INTRUDER

❖

James may have been an up-and-coming preacher, but he had a long way to go before he could emulate such men as Willie Mullan and Frank Knox. The Reverend Ian Paisley was bursting on to the scene at that time and during the 1960's would also become an effective preacher.

Mullan and Knox were spiritual giants of their particular denominations during their generation. Indeed, the pastor says the land was full of great preachers. He mentions Sam Workman who filled the Congregational Church at Newtownabbey to capacity and helped to get it out of debt, as an example.

Generally speaking, the evangelical state of the country at that time was reasonably healthy, though as the pastor came into prominence in 1957 the same could not be said of the Whitewell area.

He insists that most of the churches were full of religion and nothing else, but such a situation made James all the more determined to succeed. He had come to Whitewell to build a work that would not only reach the community but the country as a whole.

Due to his strong stance for the truth, he was looked upon as an intruder. Everyone was guarding their own patch and even today he is still considered by some as an intruder. He holds tent missions and gospel rallies in areas which have their own evangelical and pentecostal churches and often receives criticism for this. "What the critics don't consider is that I am not trying to establish a church in their area ... my only desire is to win souls for the Lord Jesus Christ," says James.

Recalling those early days on the Whitewell Road he admits that some people actually pitied him. They thought that he would be a seven-day wonder, but the fact that he is still in the area today is a testimony to the sincerity of his ministry.

He doesn't describe himself as a theologian but when he graced the pulpit to preach, things began to happen. It was clear that all of those hours spent around God's word as a young boy were not a waste of time. His congregation were of like faith, born again in every sense of the word. They were captivated by his rugged and honest style of preaching, that so often had a ball of fire attached to it.

There was no doubt that, even as a 20-year-old, Pastor James McConnell was burning with holy fire, but some of the local clergy were determined to have him burn with shame.

He was not college-trained, so they began to castigate him as nothing more than a heretic. It was bitter denunciation. They made false accusations against him.

It was then that James had no other comforter but the Lord Himself. He began to read literature about the Bible and studied God's word as never before. His personal library began to expand as he invested in works like Matthew Henry, Spurgeon, Jowett and Morrison, not to mention a host of the Puritans.

Behind this campaign of slander lay a hidden reason for the accusations. From a boy, James had been a member of the pentecostal fundamentalist group - the Church of God. They in common with the existing pentecostal church groupings had their roots in the great pentecostal visitation and out-pouring of the Holy Spirit, of which 1904 was the best known date.

The Church of God was not the result of a split or a division of any other pentecostal group of churches. The organisation was not an import from America. There was no contact with any American group when they were first founded. Instead the movement was formed with the intention of encouraging young men and women to have a deeper knowledge of God's Word. This group of people was drawn from various denominations.

Started by Pastors Forsythe and Magee in a hall in East Belfast, the Church of God expanded over the years to areas of West and South Belfast and some years later Pastor McConnell was also up and running in the Whitewell Orange Hall. During that time, however, the Church of God began to lean towards controversial doctrinal issues and began to change their original doctrinal views.

Despite this, the pastor loved the leaders within the Church of God and recognised, too, that the preachers of the movement were men who loved the Lord - particularly his two great friends Pastor James Forsythe and Pastor Gordon Magee. It was mainly for this reason that James continued within the Church of God. He even admits that things went from strength to strength in a spiritual sense for him. He didn't always fully agree with the doctrinal emphasis of the Church of God; nevertheless, he remained affiliated to them for many years, while continuing to preach faithfully in his own church at Whitewell.

It was not an easy decision to separate from the Church of God, but James believed that the Lord was leading him out of that organisation as they had become far too focused on doctrinal issues, and had lost the vision of outreach and the church planting which was their original conviction. He realised he had to come away from that type of controversy and teaching and so it was with great reluctance and after much prayer that he finally separated from them.

The bottom line for Pastor James McConnell and the church at Whitewell was that they needed their own identity. Up to that point the pastor believed the Whitewell ministry was overshadowed by the identity of the Church of God and its doctrinal stance. The people of this country didn't really know what Whitewell stood for. James felt he had to make a stand for the doctrine of the Trinity.

That stand was a belief in Calvinistic theology, namely, in God's sovereign grace. James had been a Calvinist from boyhood and still accepts those doctrines of grace. He made it known that he believed that God elects men unto salvation, and that Christ died for all of the sins of his elect. He further believed that our names have been written in the Lamb's book of life from the foundation of the world.

The issue of Calvinism has been controversial among Christians for centuries, but it's commonly conceded by many evangelicals that the brunt of the argument centres around the fact that while God saves his elect, man does have some responsibility concerning his own salvation.

It's imperative to point out that, like Spurgeon, James had never been a hyper-Calvinist. These people believe that the gospel should be preached only to men and women who know that they have a need of Christ.

This has never been the approach of Pastor McConnell, who has always followed Christ's command, "go ye into all the world and preach the gospel to every creature." For him true evangelism is giving everyone an opportunity to be saved, no matter what their background may be.

Nevertheless, back in the late fifties and sixties it wasn't easy to convince the people of Northern Ireland of his sincerity regarding the truth. He was seen by many as a ministerial fake and received unwelcome publicity from the local media.

In recent years the pastor has received what may be regarded as good publicity, due to the phenomenal growth of the Whitewell church. But in those early days not all of the news about him was good. He was entering the public eye and, as he did so, reports true and false began to surface in the local newspapers. In one or two articles he recalls how they made fun of the church, especially about Whitewell's missionary endeavours, but added, "People who make fun like that, without the facts, don't know what they are talking about."

In the main, he tried hard not to respond to the defamatory remarks. He prefers to live by the motto, "no defence, no attack," a policy he says has kept his heart free from bitterness.

Opposition or not, this intruder was here to stay and a great work was about to begin.

Chapter Thirteen

BUILDING PROJECT

❖

I t was the mid 1960's when James attempted his first major
building project. By then it had become evident that as
a church Whitewell would have to purchase a spiritual
home of its own, as the Orange Hall wasn't large enough to
accommodate all who wanted to attend.

Ground was purchased and plans passed as the Whitewell
brethren, both young and old, began working on a first sanctuary. They soon ran into problems.

As the site was situated on a hill, it had to be excavated.
The excavators went so close to the adjoining property that the
owners panicked and threatened court action. They believed
their property was on the verge of collapse and were most
unhappy with the situation.

The architect was called in to design a retaining wall that
would go around the entire site.

The cost was estimated at £2,500, a small fortune in those
days, especially for a congregation which was still only seventy
in number. Despite an increasing interest level in his preaching,

only a few people who attended the Orange Hall were genuine members. When the project hit financial problems, the wheat was separated from the chaff even further as the congregation numbers declined to just forty.

Many made excuses and left, but the sacrifice and giving of those remaining forty warriors was outstanding. Some of the members gave the pastor all of their wages, not just one week, but many weeks. It was 1968 and the church was collecting approximately £300.00 each week, perhaps about £30,000 in today's money.

Every day from early morning brethren met at that site. Supervised by brother John McCallister, they were determined by the grace of God to build a house dedicated to the Lord Jesus Christ.

As for Pastor McConnell, those days were a time of much activity as he continued to lead by example. His members knew he was a man who could preach, but they were beginning to see the Holy Spirit at work in his life, making him into a man compelled to go the extra mile.

But life wasn't always taken so seriously by his members and he was often the brunt of practical jokes. There were many humorous and memorable moments. One afternoon while giving a hand at the site, the pastor began to sink in muddy sand, and he had to be rescued by his brethren. If ever a chorus of "From sinking sand he lifted me" was appropriate, it was at that particular moment.

The work continued unabated for over two years. John McCallister and his helpers could be seen at that first site, digging, mixing cement, carrying bricks and negotiating with sub-contractors to get the best price, as did the pastor. When it transpired that the Whitewell people had to carry out further excavation work, Pastor McConnell encouraged his flock by example and all problems were overcome.

He believed that if Jesus the Son of God had to work, then there was no sacrifice too great for himself and his congregation to make. He motivated his tired but faithful brethren with the words of Jesus in the book of John, "My Father worketh hitherto and I work." John 5:17.

It was labour that paid off as he and his loyal band of men and women, not forgetting the children, finally completed the project and moved into a beautiful new building (not far from the Orange Hall) on April 5th, 1969.

What had seemed impossible had come to pass and remarkably with something to spare, as together they had raised £30,000. Having spent the previous twelve years in a rented hall, the new facility was like a cathedral. Complete with a small balcony, it seated 450 people and was a marvellous expression of God's faithfulness to those who are faithful to him.

Another chapter was about to unfold in the remarkable history of the Whitewell Church. Throughout those early years, God had said to the pastor and his committed congregation what Christ himself had said to the Ephesian Church in Revelation 2:2. "I know thy labour."

Real labour, however, was just beginning - as was the success of the Metropolitan Church, Belfast.

Chapter Fourteen

TROUBLED TIMES

❖

The new cathedral was a place where God was about to send forth his Holy Spirit in a way that had not been previously experienced.

It wasn't quite a national revival like the Welsh one in 1859, it was more a local one.

First, though, it is important to set the scene in the province of Ulster at that time. Since the eruption of violence back in 1968, Northern Ireland has, of course, experienced social and political turmoil.

Its capital, Belfast, is a city where war has found a comfortable home.

Established buildings, at the beginning of the nineteen seventies, became, by the end of the decade, heaps of rubble and fallen telephone lines. The troubles have since become a bitter and bloody conflict, in which many innocent civilians and children have been murdered.

During the early years of the first church at Whitewell, life outside it was anything but normal. Bombs were exploding at

random, in shops, hotels and public buildings, all over Belfast.
Provincial towns were affected, too, particularly by car bombs.
These were commonplace, and often exploded without
warning. Hundreds were murdered, either as members of the
security forces, or as civilians. The horrifying part of this was
that many of them were shot in view of their closest colleagues
or families.

Therefore the year 1969 signalled more than just the
beginning of Whitewell's first church; it was also the year that
the troubles began in earnest ... thus influencing an entire
generation.

Paradoxes abound in Northern Ireland. One is the peace-
fulness of the place. Although no town or village has been
unaffected, the worst of the violence has been localised and the
motto might well be "Business as usual."

So, despite the fact that many of the Whitewell members
were affected by the troubles, the church has since clung to that
very same motto.

Those early days were fraught with danger, particularly
due to the fact that the church was situated in the centre of a
mixed community and North Belfast became a hot-bed of
hatred.

There were times when you could have cut the atmosphere
with a knife, and the situation had escalated to such a frighten-
ing level for Pastor McConnell and his congregation, that on
two separate occasions there were gun battles outside the
church. During one of these battles, when many members were
locked inside, terrorists fired at the army and imbedded in the
ceiling of that first sanctuary are bullets from those ferocious
attacks.

The biggest shock, however, was during the month of
August. As members of the Whitewell Church set off on their
annual Sunday School excursion, they were told by police to
return early as information suggested the church might be blown
up by terrorists.

Having spent those previous years labouring to build their
new sanctuary, such news came as a devastating blow to James
McConnell and his congregation. The thought of that most

precious house going up in smoke was not easily contemplated.

As has always been the case during the Ulster troubles, security forces could not offer any real protection, as outbreaks of violence had stretched resources to the full. The facts were that they were being pulled in so many different directions that they simply couldn't cope.

The Whitewell people were angry. The pastor also. They were not going to accept these threats. Many decided to keep a daily vigil at the church, so the members slept overnight, prepared for any attack. They even had sand, hoses and water at the ready, but by the grace of God the night passed off peacefully.

The faith of many during this time was certainly tested as sectarian violence, bloodshed and bombing reached unprecedented levels. Members living in flashpoint areas were frightened to come out as buses were being hijacked and set on fire.

One particular night some of the young people of the church were attending a prayer meeting when gunfire erupted outside the premises. The pastor, on hearing of this, rushed down to the church but was stopped by a soldier. Once the pastor had explained why he wanted through, he was allowed to reach the doors of the sanctuary. To his surprise, when he entered the hall, twelve of the youngsters had been baptised in the Holy Spirit. One of these was his daughter Linda.

They hadn't even been aware of the conflict outside.

Certainly it was a most difficult time for the pastor to be preaching the truth, but preach he did. Despite threatening phone calls to his home, he refused to remain silent. With a significant escalation in violence and lawlessness in the community, it was essential to speak loudly and clearly on the subject of peace and justice.

James sought the Lord like never before. Some people, including the police, thought he was going crazy. The police landrover would often pick him up walking the streets late at night.

"Where are you going?" they would ask.

"I'm seeking God," James replied.

The police, who got to know him well, always had the last word.

"Come on, hop in and let's go home," they would say.

Out of the chaos, however, God was about to bring a 'local revival.'

The first way in which God used the troubles as a catalyst to build His church was in the emergence of the Whitewell bus ministry. It was born out of sheer necessity. Members had literally no other way of reaching the church due to the demise of a regular bus service in the city.

Subsequently the idea to instigate their own independent service was an instant success and it has grown ever since.

Back then, though, in 1969, the country was plummeting to an all-time low and the church seemed powerless to bring an end to the bloodshed.

Congregations which attended the first church at Whitewell didn't exceed 150 and the pastor became tired and frustrated by life in Northern Ireland during this period.

A wave of discontentment came over him: something just had to be done. Against the advice of certain members, he renewed his old habit of walking, praying and knocking at doors, regardless of political or religious background. These were years of tremendous labour, yet wonderful blessing. Despite the troubles, the next three years saw a period of constant witnessing, not to mention prayer meetings six days a week.

At times it was discouraging as the work seemed void of reward.

However … a dramatic change was coming.

Chapter Fifteen

SUPERNATURAL VISITATION

❖

September 1973 is still remembered as an amazing month in the life of Pastor James McConnell, one he describes as the turning point in the history of the Whitewell Church. Yet unknown to him and his congregation, it was also the beginning of the supernatural at Whitewell.

The same messenger that had visited Pastor McConnell's home many times, his office at the shipyard, and his church in Newcastle, returned to direct his steps.

Pastor McConnell had been seeking the Lord. He announced to his flock one particular Sunday morning that he hadn't been called to be the keeper of an aquarium, but to be a fisher of men. He also announced that he had been walking for miles and praying in a way that he had never known before. He asked the people to kindly refrain from calling at the church during the week, as he felt something unusual was about to happen. But members continued to see his car parked outside and called, despite his plea not to. Things got so bad that he parked the car in a different place, and walked to the church, but the people still visited.

One day he found solace. It was while standing on the small balcony of the church that the Angel of the Lord came down and stood with him. It was not a vision, nor a dream, for the pastor was wide awake and fully conscious. By his own admission he had seen this messenger many times and he always appeared in the form of a man.

The Angel told him how he wanted the sinner's prayer to be prayed as well as many other things, but most significantly he told him that, from that point on, every time James would preach the gospel, souls would be saved. For those who don't believe in modern-day miracles, it's now almost a quarter of a century since that visitation and every Lord's day since, without a single break, many souls spanning every age group and denomination have been converted to Christ.

A prophecy followed which said,

"Have you love? Prepare to receive those from the dunghill; the rejects of society. Love and receive them as I have you."

Following that great visitation Pastor McConnell was rejuvenated. After the visitation his prayers took legs and his preaching took wings. He had more love, compassion, encouragement and exhortation in his character than ever before. Since then he has preached out against sin in a much more authoritative way.

But the pastor was not the only one within the Whitewell Church at that time to see the messenger of the Lord. Many people claim to have seen the cloud of the Lord. One particular Sunday evening a number of people, who were strangers to each other, came to the pastor afterwards convinced they had seen an Angel on the gallery of the church. Was the pastor surprised at this? "Not at all," says Pastor McConnell, "I had sighted it myself on a number of occasions, but hadn't made it public."

The light of the Lord is another sight many of those early worshippers were privileged to see. For example, one particular Sunday morning a young couple brought their baby to be dedicated in full view of their family circle. As the pastor took the child in his arms to bless it, he saw a tremendous light descend upon a young man in the balcony, as did many other members. At that point, the same boy ran out into the hall, fell on his face and gave his life to Jesus Christ.

Stories abound of the way in which God moved in that first church, despite the troubles. There was the time Pastor McConnell was told by the Holy Spirit to visit a man called Mr. Howard in the Royal Victoria Hospital before ten o'clock that evening and point him to Christ. The pastor was told by the spirit to be no later than 10 pm. Immediately he made his way to the hospital, but found that every gate was locked. Somehow he managed to get through army barricades and eventually spoke to the man in question. After a short conversation, Mr. Howard admitted that he needed Jesus as he had cancer and was dying. It was then that the pastor, kneeling by the bedside, led him to Christ. Remarkably, as he stood up and looked at the clock, it was exactly ten o'clock.

Another supernatural account is recalled by one of the Metropolitan Church's longest serving pastors, William McTernaghan. He has been with Pastor McConnell from the very beginning of the Whitewell ministry and has seen hundreds of evidences of the supernatural. Yet he has no doubt about the incident that stands out for him.

His father took a massive heart attack and while lying in the ambulance was pronounced dead. When they arrived at the hospital, he somehow regained consciousness and told Pastor McConnell that he didn't think he was going to live. Immediately the pastor said, "Thus saith the Holy Ghost you will live for another 15 years."

Pastor McTernaghan added,

"I didn't believe it but my dad made a full recovery and went on for years until one day he took a severe cold and consequently felt very poorly. He informed the whole family that it was exactly 15 years since his heart attack and that God would be taking him home shortly.

He called for Pastor McConnell, who, when informed of this, told my dad that God might give him an extension on the 15 years. Remarkably, though, my dad passed away that very week … exactly 15 years from the time the pastor had spoken to him by the Spirit."

One of the most memorable experiences of Pastor McConnell's entire ministry occurred as the members of his church were preparing for a gospel mission at the Oval, home of Glentoran Football Club.

Two of his workers came and asked the pastor to call round and see a Catholic woman, who was suffering from cancer. She had asked for Pastor McConnell as she knew him to be a saved man and, even though she didn't attend his church, she respected his walk with God.

"Have you anything you can comfort me with?" she asked the pastor, after he arrived at her home.

At that point the Holy Spirit came to his rescue with the words of John chapter 14. In fact, he quoted the whole chapter from memory. Then he re-read the words from the twenty-seventh verse, 'Peace I leave with you, my peace I give unto you, not as the world giveth, give I unto you, let not your heart be troubled, neither let it be afraid.'

The woman expressed her thanks and told the pastor that those were the words she was searching for in her time of need.

Then they both got down on their knees and the lady accepted Christ as her personal Saviour. Her whole life was changed, and Pastor McConnell had the joy, if only briefly, of seeing this woman attend his church meetings.

Three weeks later, she invited the pastor to her home and stunned him by asking him to take her funeral as she was being called home by the Lord that night. Naturally he concluded that God was not taking her home, but that she was merely exaggerating. The lady insisted, however, and again she made the pastor promise that he would take her funeral later that week. The pastor was then moved to tears as the woman began to quote from John chapter 14, just as he had done a few weeks beforehand. She completed the entire chapter from memory, but amazingly by midnight she had passed away just as she said she would.

It is still a significant and amazing event, one of the greatest the pastor has ever witnessed.

On another occasion, Pastor McConnell was being driven to the town of Antrim by Pastor Bertie Blake. As they approached the town centre, Pastor McConnell asked to be taken back to the Rathcoole Estate.

Pastor Blake explains why.

"I thought he had lost his senses, but he assured me that the Spirit of God had spoken to him and that he was needed immediately at the home of a man called Sammy Campbell."

Sammy's wife, Dolly, is still a member of the Whitewell Church and takes up the story:

"When the car arrived, Sammy was lying in a deep coma. Doctors said there was no way he would recover and that death was certain. The medical people wanted to close the doors of the ambulance, but Pastor McConnell persuaded them not to. After a few minutes of prayer, and to the amazement of everyone, Sammy opened his eyes and began to cry. The pastor asked him if he wanted to come to the Lord and he agreed. After he had got right with God he slipped back into the coma and passed away. It was a miracle of God," says Dolly.

Pastor Blake, who is regarded as Pastor McConnell's closest friend since the passing away of Gordon Magee, points out that, although the Whitewell people have seen and heard about so many supernatural events, it is still something they cannot get used to.

He says, "I believe in miracles, because I have seen too many of them not to believe. I have seen people in Whitewell healed of terrible diseases like cancers, tumours and all kinds of deadly infections. The Whitewell people have witnessed the casting out of demons according to scripture and have known a multitude of other healings to take place.

God is a supernatural God and the God of miracles. The only reason that it is not the norm today is that people have little faith. We at Whitewell believe that Jesus Christ is the same yesterday, today and forever. If Jesus Christ is not the same Jesus that he was when he was on earth, then the gospel cannot be the same," insists Pastor Blake.

As the troubles in Ulster continued to escalate, there's no doubt that members of Whitewell experienced at first hand what Christ had promised to His disciples in the book of Mark, "And these signs shall follow those who believe; In my name they shall cast out devils, they shall speak with new tongues, they shall take up serpents, and if they drink anything deadly it shall not hurt them. They shall lay hands on the sick and they shall recover."

The people of that first house could relate fully, in fact, to the words of the Psalmist, "Thou art the God that doest wonders: Thou hast declared thy strength among the people." Psalm 77:14.

Indeed, such is the sheer volume of wonder-working testimonies during this period, it would be impossible to adequately describe the remarkable events which took place in that first sanctuary known as the "Little church with the spire."

Chapter Sixteen

IT'LL NEVER STOP

❖

When George Stephenson made the first steam engine he invited his sister Mary to see it. She looked at it, and then commented to her brother, "It'll never go." George replied, "Get in." Again his sister answered, "It'll never go."

"Get in and we will see," said George defiantly.

Finally his sister reluctantly agreed.

After Mary got in, the whistle blew and there was a puff of smoke and the engine started off. It was then that Mary cried out, "It'll never stop! It'll never stop!"

As literally hundreds of new worshippers began to throng into the little church at the bottom of the Whitewell Road, Pastor James McConnell was about to experience the same feeling as Stephenson.

Years of preparation in the wilderness were now over. From telling himself many times, when trying to kick-start his church, "It'll never go, it'll never go," the pastor suddenly found himself uttering the words, "It'll never stop."

The 'Pentecostal revival' the pastor had desired from those early days in the Orange Hall had arrived, even if it was, by his own admission, a local revival. Numbers soared from 150 to almost 700 people as the Whitewell church was packed to capacity. Those assembling exceeded even the pastor's greatest expectations. He couldn't believe it.

Every seat was taken as worshippers saturated the aisles and blocked the front door. Many stood outside, hoping for a sighting of the pastor in the full flood of his sermon. For the first time in its history, the Whitewell Church needed extra chairs and space as converts came in their hundreds.

Observers in the neighbourhood were fascinated to find crowds spilling over on to the streets. Considering this was during the troubles, it was a miracle of God.

Miracle or not, word continued to spread about the kind of visitation the church had received.

People from various backgrounds converged. Among them were religious people, working and middle-class citizens and those curious to find out just what was going on. Many ministers were puzzled as to why James had become so popular. Other men who had attended Bible College and attained academic and religious qualifications were not receiving similar blessings ... indeed by comparison their churches were virtually empty.

Thus the popularity, even the status of Pastor McConnell, irritated certain individuals. They began to ridicule him again. He was the 'talk of the town' as the saying goes, but when people arrived to hear him preach they soon realised that most of the talk was utter nonsense.

They had heard an evil report, yet his preaching was honest, pure and true. It was delivered in what Belfast folk describe as 'shipyard language', as his messages were always easy to understand.

Almost immediately an influx of terrorists, alcoholics, prostitutes, drug addicts, and homosexuals - both Catholic and Protestant - began to descend on the church. Just as the Angel had promised, people in distress, debt or desperation came and the Lord Jesus became a captain over them.

Taunts were levelled against Whitewell as to the type of people that were being brought to the church. Yet the Whitewell congregation have continually sought to be guided by Scripture, and were only doing what our Lord had taught the multitudes in Matthew 25:35-36.

"For I was hungry and you gave me food; I was a stranger and you took me in; I was naked and you clothed me; I was sick and you visited me; I was in prison and you came to me."

The pastor and his flock were fed-up with formal religion in Ulster. They wanted a church which practised true Christianity, a church which was not disingenuous or shallow. Moreover, those early members wanted a church that had received a baptism of real love. They took literally the words of Matthew 28:19 "Go ye therefore and make disciples of all nations, baptising them in the name of the Father, the Son and the Holy Ghost, teaching them to observe all things which I have commanded you."

Friends and well-meaning people warned the pastor about accepting people who were regarded as "trashy." But the pastor soon found out, as did Spurgeon after he helped similar kinds of converts, that the so-called "trash" often turned out to be the "cream of the crop."

By now, however, the pastor had left behind his old style of preaching which in his own words was, 'dour, dull and dogmatic.' "It was typical of the early 'sixties style', but without any real bite," he says.

During the start of his ministry he admits to cultivating the techniques of other preachers, resulting in a loss of direction for a period of time.

Despite this, he has always endeavoured to maintain great reverence for God in the pulpit, being constantly aware of the massive responsibility that comes with the preaching of the gospel.

From his earliest recollections James has never tolerated irreverence during the services. On the contrary, women and children sprint for their lives for fear of disrupting a meeting and receiving the wrath of his tongue. One observer remarked after a particular Lord's Day meeting:

"I have never heard a preacher who commands so much respect." Then he added, "He doesn't suffer fools gladly, does he?"

It's recorded that C. H. Spurgeon rarely met his congregation face to face after a service; by comparison, however, James had always been available before and after his preaching to minister to the needs of his flock. He doesn't see a preacher as someone who goes into the pulpit and appears as God: he sees himself simply as a man with a message.

Here again we have evidence of balance in his ministry. No airs or graces, but, equally, no lack of sincerity either. How he loved to worship and pray in those early days, but it was his preaching that became the focal point of everything he did. It characterised his entire ministry.

When he preached on the parables of Jesus Christ, he made them very real. When he spoke about Bible characters, it was like watching a movie rather than listening to a sermon and it is even more like that today. He became a very Christ-centred preacher, able to preach on any subject from the Bible. It seemed that when he preached about the life of our Lord Jesus Christ the Bible came alive to everyone and it was no surprise that thousands of Ulster people came to Christ in that first church as a result of his ministry.

Thousands of Pastor McConnell's sermons have been recorded over the years, many worthy of mention. All of them have one thing in common, however. They conclude with a genuine invitation to come to Christ. Many of his congregation agree that this part of the sermon highlights best their pastor's obvious love for his Saviour Jesus Christ. Known as the appeal, Pastor McConnell searches relentlessly for sinners in need of repentance. He confronts them with the great issue of salvation and matters pertaining to their souls. To him their souls are of paramount importance and he is determined by the grace of God to win them for Christ.

In fact, unless one attended a Sunday evening service, it would be difficult to appreciate the passion he puts into his closing appeal. But we can glean something of the tremendous compassion he had for lost souls back in that first church, and still retains today, by recalling the last part of one of those early addresses.

"Love is a gift from God and God has put within everyone of you a soul tonight. That's why Jesus said, 'What shall it profit a man if he should gain the whole world and lose his own soul … or what shall a man give in exchange for his soul.' Oh listen, friend, what has got to happen in your life tonight to make you realise that you need God; what has got to happen in your family for you to realise that you need Christ? Without Christ in your life you are useless and lost. You have no direction and I implore you to come to that place - the place where you look up at the middle cross at Calvary, smitten with precious blood, and see on that cross God's Son, the pivot on whom the whole world and universe rests, and say to Him, I believe that you are the Son of God and I believe that you died for me; take my life and live in me. Friend, if you do that, Christ will come and save you for time and eternity and he will make you his own. He will lift you from the dunghill and set you among princes. Can I hear an Amen? I repeat, he will lift you from the dunghill, but if you want to stay on your dunghill, then stay there, because that dunghill will be removed into a lost eternity to be doomed and damned and lost and separated eternally from the presence of God. Oh to be a sinner saved by sovereign grace and by the blood of our Lord Jesus Christ."

As hundreds of people responded to this invitation by raising their hands to acknowledge Christ, many criticised this early method of appeal, which is still used today in the new Tabernacle. But the pastor defends such a method. "Putting a hand up doesn't save a person," says the pastor. "Signing a book, even becoming a member of the church can't save anyone. Only the blood of Jesus Christ can do that.

"But the raising of a person's hand is important for two reasons. It shows they are serious about coming to Christ. They have publicly identified with their Saviour. Also it helps the church deacons and brethren to be more aware of those who have just accepted the Lord Jesus Christ in order to encourage them."

The rising numbers were welcomed, but this meant that Whitewell as a church would never be the same again. Gone was the little homely assembly. Suddenly the Pastor was in constant demand by his congregation to the extent that he had to change his original daily schedule. He had to scrap weekly counselling and deal with people as soon as they came to Christ. That's not to say that he wasn't available for those in need, but such was the flood of converts that he had to employ other pastors who would pay them a visit during the week and take them under their wing for a while.

Having said this, James had always believed that the guidance of new converts is more the Lord's task. His attitude is that if a new convert is serious about coming to Christ, he will go on with God. Pastors are there to comfort and counsel, but unless men and women have a desire to get right with God all the counselling in the world is just a waste of time.

There would be further trial and error. Not all the conversions were lasting ones, indeed only about one in four grew to maturity. Regarding the marks of true conversion the pastor has always been guided by scripture, and in particular the words of the gospel of Mark:

"The precious seed falls on four kinds of ground: the wayside: the stony: the thorny and the good."

Such an influx of true converts, however, filled the pastor with great satisfaction. For years he had dreamed about revival, but to realise it, even in embryonic form, was an experience he relished. Yet he was still totally unaware of what the Holy Spirit was planning for the years which lay ahead.

The movement of the Spirit was gaining momentum.

Chapter Seventeen

BUILDING AGAIN

❖

For the next twenty years crowds would continue to grow. As 800 worshippers attempted to get into the 700 capacity church, the words "It'll never stop," were most appropriate.

The idea of yet another new church was prompted after two walls were knocked down to increase the capacity to over 800, but still they came in their hundreds. One Sunday evening there were at least 1,000 people, many of whom had to stay outside. Like Spurgeon said of the success of his New Park Street Church, "It was like pouring the Atlantic Ocean into a teapot."

It was time to build again ... time to seek planning permission for a sanctuary that would hold 1,500 people. Certainly the purchasing of that ground is a remarkable tale and one that the pastor is still amazed at.

One morning, the presence of the Lord came upon James and said, 'Prepare yourself today. A man is coming to meet you concerning the new ground - offer him £15,000.'

After waiting at the church all day, however, no one showed up and immediately he thought he had imagined the whole thing. It was while watching the news at six o'clock that a man called at his house willing to sell him a plot of land for £18,000.

The pastor then said, "I have been told to give you £15,000."

"Who told you?" asked the man.

James replied, "Headquarters."

The sale was agreed and the rest is history.

It was yet again proof that the Spirit of God was with him, and despite being separated unto the gospel, Pastor McConnell still found time to encourage hundreds of those early converts. As his dear wife Margaret said of him, he became a good shepherd over them.

Once again, together with his colleagues and congregation, James was back digging foundations and mixing cement. Like the first site, the fellowship and comradeship never waned and in just three years by a miracle of God the new house was erected. Ironically the move came after a period of twelve years - the same amount of time which was spent in the Orange Hall. During this time two more men came into full-time service and the highly successful bus fleet was increased in size.

Missionary endeavours soared, too, as Whitewell entered an exciting new era. The capacity of the second church changed to 1,500 and there would eventually be a change in the name of the church. The new title would be: "The Metropolitan Church, Whitewell."

The new house was officially opened at the end of October, 1981.

It's worth mentioning that if the contractor had built and priced it, the cost would have been £1.6 million. Instead the Whitewell congregation raised the money and built it themselves for £800,000 - a tremendous achievement in what was a period of recession, inflation and unemployment. In that financial year they gave £261,508.

Add to this the fact that the church was also supporting a fleet of buses, their own missionaries in Spain, the persecuted church behind the Iron Curtain, a large tape ministry and many other activities. Their sense of achievement in officially opening another new house was certainly justified.

Other ministers might have been content with such an accomplishment, but not Pastor James McConnell. He was determined to evangelise his church, the immediate area and the entire countryside.

In fact, the desire for lost souls in his life became so great a burden upon him that he constantly encouraged his members to knock doors, distribute tracts and preach God's word in many areas of this troubled province of Ulster.

It is a compassion for God's people which has constantly kept Pastor McConnell out of the political spotlight. Unlike many secular politicians, he still believes that "Jesus is the only answer" to the political problems of the Northern Ireland conflict.

Inevitably over the years such a strong stance for the truth has merited its fair share of publicity. The main reason, however, for increased media attention which began to emerge at this time was not just the erecting of two large churches in the space of 12 years, but also because of the unique gathering within Whitewell of both Protestants and Catholics, worshipping together in peace and in love.

Up to this point the pastor and his people had seen miracles of all kinds, but when the Holy Spirit told the servant of God that both religions would start coming together through Christ it seemed hard to believe. After all, political polarisation was at its peak. Sectarian hatred was at its maximum, too, while Christian love and unity was at an all-time low.

As great Lord's Day services continued with hundreds of souls being won for Christ, the Holy Spirit threw down a fresh challenge.

The question was ... could the pastor and his people respond?

Chapter Eighteen

MAN WITH A MISSION

❖

"Fill the King's Hall in Belfast and preach the gospel." That was the message from the Holy Spirit to Pastor James McConnell and his assembly.

The hall held 8,000, and nothing similar had ever before been attempted by his church.

Such faith was encouraged by the fact that God had been working mightily within the new Metropolitan Church at this time. No fewer than 60 people came to Christ after one particular Sunday night healing service in what marked the beginning of an awesome period of soul winning.

It was while stopped in traffic outside the King's Hall that the pastor first thought about going to what is still one of Belfast's largest entertainment complexes. He saw thousands streaming out after hearing the pop singer Elton John and the Holy Spirit whispered to him: "Do you think you could fill that place?"

His reply was, "No, Lord, but you could fill it."

The pastor never had any doubts that God would answer him and his faith was rewarded. On Sunday, 31st March, 1985, 9,000 people packed into the King's Hall to hear him preach.

The manager of the building said the turnout was a fantastic achievement. He was a man called Mr. Rees and, not surprisingly, he was sceptical beforehand about the whole idea, commenting at the time, "I don't think you will be able to fill the hall."

He was happy to be proved wrong, though.

The evening cost around £20,000 to promote while an incredible 450,000 handbills were delivered. But after 250 persons responded to the pastor's message entitled, "Being ashamed of Christ," all thoughts of cost and effort vanished. 205 people were redeemed by the blood of Jesus, although it is still estimated that around 370 people raised their hands that night to acknowledge their need of Christ .

Interestingly, it wasn't just the pastor who benefited from the spin-off of new members. Many other ministers telephoned him at this time to tell him they had new converts in their churches and naturally they were absolutely delighted.

Making his debut at the country's international soccer venue, Windsor Park, had been James McConnell's goal since he was a schoolboy, but even he could not have dreamed that his first full appearance there would be as a minister of the gospel.

The ground was also the home of his favourite boyhood team, Linfield F.C., and a place he had visited many times during his youth.

After the success of the King's Hall event, James was determined to double that attendance with the Windsor rally on June 16th, 1985, under the banner "The Champion of Champions - Jesus."

People predicted that the King's Hall event would be a failure, but in the end so many people turned up that they were standing in the aisles. This gave the pastor the encouragement he needed prior to the Windsor Park event, one which he believed would be the biggest ever.

His intention was to address the crowd from a nine-foot stage erected at the old Spion Kop at the end of the ground. The Spion Kop has since been demolished in favour of a new all-seater stand. Around the pastor, on three sides, the congregation was to be packed into the newly-built £2 million north stand, the much older south stand at the far end of the pitch, and the railway stand.

Over £10,000 was invested in the form of handbills, posters and the hire of a giant platform, but you can imagine the shock when news broke that the Whitewell Church was not allowed to hold a gospel mission at Linfield's ground. This was due to repercussions following the Bradford City Football Club fire disaster which prompted new legislation. People perished in the flames at Bradford when their wooden stand caught fire and immediately the Football Association ordered that every grandstand of every stadium should be inspected. Thus the south stand of Linfield Football Club, which held 3,500 people, was declared unsafe and unfit.

Immediately the telephones started to ring. The BBC and UTV beamed out the controversial story at peak viewing time. The Belfast Telegraph's front page read, "Church slams IFA red tape."

The News Letter's headline read: "Rally at soccer pitch offside."

Another read: "Pastor sticks to rally plans, despite grandstand shock."

Every day the papers, radio and television highlighted the way the pastor and his people were treated by the authorities. At first this publicity was of great concern and the pastor initially wondered if God really had told him to go to Windsor Park. God soon confirmed that the rally was of Him by reminding His servant that He had brought the Whitewell Church and its message to the attention of the nation.

The pastor instantly launched one final effort to get the south stand open. Meetings at Stormont buildings were organised, where he met with the Reverend Ian Paisley and Sir Nicholas Scott. The government minister was unable to help, however, as there was a legal clause preventing any intervention.

The only way the rally could go ahead now was if people sat out in the open. "What if it rains?" thought the pastor, who eventually consulted his brethren about the idea. To a man they agreed to chance it and hundreds of chairs were transported from the church to the venue.

It appeared every obstacle had now been removed. The last advertisement read, 'Ulster people to solve Ulster's problems. It's on - presenting the champion of champions, the Lord Jesus Christ.' There was still another hurdle to climb, however. One that the pastor had precious little experience in dealing with.

During the week before the Windsor Park event, he woke one morning at around 4.30 am. Soaked with perspiration, he began to walk around the house shouting aloud. It was clear he was having a nightmare or vision after the dramatic events of the past month when the IFA's closure of grandstands created such a high profile for his church. He dreamed he was in the middle of the pitch crying at people.

"Christ loves you and there is nothing He cannot do for you."

Suddenly a dark figure towered above him and replied: 'This land belongs to me, I'll never let you have it.'

The pastor felt his shoulders being grabbed by this powerful figure. It was so real that he felt pain sweeping through his whole body.

"Who are you?" asked James.

As he continued to walk he heard a voice in the dark saying: "I am the prince of this land."

James was completely drained. Like Daniel he could say, "Therefore I was left alone, and saw this great vision, and there remained no strength in me." (Dan 10:8) He had been put in a position where he was not equal to the task, so that God could make up the difference - and this He did.

Regardless of the red tape the rally went ahead and suddenly the headlines changed to, "Pastor's sermon is heard by thousands as hands unite across the divide." A crowd of 12,000, three thousand short of what had been anticipated, heard that sermon, but it was still the biggest congregation James had ever addressed.

Whitewell's vision of faith and hope had united Protestant and Catholic in the unlikely setting of a football stadium. People from as far as Dublin, Dundalk, Newry and Crossmaglen flocked to Windsor Park that day and over 200 souls from every religious persuasion came to Christ.

Out of the darkness of the troubles God had brought light and unity to a land which for so long had known nothing but division. As the Scripture says, "And that He might reconcile them both to God in one body through the cross, having slain the enmity thereby." (Ephesians 2:16.)

That period of evangelism continued. The Metropolitan Church hired the Larne Football Club grounds as there wasn't a large enough hall in the town to accommodate all those who wanted to come and hear the gospel. The church had a challenge - the challenge of seeing more souls saved. By the end of that particular evening another thirty people had come forward for Christ. Pastor McConnell was delighted. This time there   was a crowd of just 2,500 in total, small in comparison with the Windsor Park turnout, but still a fantastic attendance given the mood of depression during the troubles.

Sadly for the people of Whitewell, however, that depression was about to deepen. Around the corner lay suffering and heartbreak.

The years of carrying their cross were by no means over.

Chapter Nineteen

THE SHADOW OF DEATH

---------------- ❖ ----------------

I t's worth remembering that this was the era when the IRA
were carrying out their policy of killing members of the
security forces by bombs, bullets and other methods.

Hundreds of civilians, too, were being murdered, yet
despite this the membership of the Whitewell Church continued to increase. Even two tragic incidents which arrived on the
doorstep of the Greencastle assembly failed to discourage the
people.

Having said that, the loss of one of their most respected
members, David Purse (senior), who was gunned down by the
IRA while on RUC duty, and the shooting of Ivan Walker, who
by a miracle of God recovered, still left many members and
friends deeply shocked.

David Purse had been with Pastor McConnell from the
very first meeting in the Orange Hall. Naturally, the news
of the tragedy stunned his wife Ann and their three boys.
Thousands attended the funeral, but out of the chaos and
suffering God was still working. David's eldest son (called

after him) was just fifteen at the time and shortly after the shooting of his dad he was singled out publicly by the Spirit of God. He was called by prophecy to prepare himself to work for the Kingdom of God.

David (junior), who is today fulfilling that prophecy, pastoring in Withernsea, England, still recalls how Pastor McConnell broke the news to him that his dad had been murdered.

"It was a Saturday afternoon and I knew something was wrong when Pastor McConnell called at the house. My dad had been policing a football game between Crusaders and Portadown and was shot while standing outside the ground. I still remember how the pastor took me to my bedroom, told me to be strong and then said.

'David, your daddy has been shot dead by the IRA.'"

The boy burst into tears and found his mum and brothers also weeping.

Naturally the young man thought it was all a bad dream. He hoped that he had fallen asleep and would waken up to find his dad alive and well. But David Purse (senior) never did come home.

In the case of Ivan Walker he, too, was an established member of the Metropolitan Church and his story is an equally remarkable testimony to the sheer power of God. Although not a saved man at the time, he attended the Metropolitan Church with his wife Betty. Ivan was a roofer by trade and it was while working on a roof-top that he was shot no fewer than nine times by the IRA. Miraculously he was still breathing, although he was in a coma for nine weeks, firstly on a life support machine and then in the intensive care unit.

The pastor visited Ivan many times and sat by his bedside. Much prayer, of course, was offered by the people of the church at this time, but then something happened.

The life support machine was stopped and Ivan was pronounced dead. People were praying for him even at that moment. Ivan tells of how he was then taken by Jesus Christ and led into the very presence of God. A voice said, "Father, I present Ivan Walker to you, will you receive him?"

At that moment he felt the cleansing power of the blood of Jesus. Then suddenly he began to breathe again and slowly but surely came back to life. After this he made a remarkable recovery, although his health has never been quite the same.

The Whitewell people were walking through the valley of the shadow of death, but like the psalmist they feared no evil. They could say, like David, "Thou art with me, thy rod and thy staff they comfort me."

Many other members were victims of the troubles, but instead of discouraging the pastor and his flock, those events stirred up the spirit within them. Goodness and mercy had followed them all of the days of their lives so far. Why would they quit now?

With committed families in his church such as these, Pastor McConnell continued his great mid-eighties mission of tracking down lost souls. He, too, refused to doubt Almighty God, who still had something left for him to do.

The biggest task of all, in fact.

The pastor inside the Metropolitan Tabernacle.

Interior view of the Sanctuary.

Dr. McConnell in the pulpit.

Dr. McConnell with his good friend, well known Ulster Evangelist, Rev. Sam Workman.

In the central foyer at the Tabernacle.

A view towards the Fountain.

Pulpit and Communion Table.

View toward the pulpit area with the Tabernacle choir in the background.

The text reminds us that in changing circumstances Jesus Christ is always the same.

The central foyer connects the main Sanctuary to the 1,200-seater hall, restaurant and administrative wing.

A mural in the central foyer.

Main entrance to the balcony.
Above the door 'Christ Centred'.

The Metropolitan Recreation Centre.

James McConnell receiving an honorary doctorate from the California Graduate School of Theology, July 1986.

The Pastor in his office at the Tabernacle.

The Metropolitan at night.

PART THREE

FILLED WITH WISDOM

Chapter Twenty

BUILDING YET AGAIN

❖

Having gone to the people of Ulster with the message of the gospel, it was now time for the people to come to the pastor.

As word travelled about his preaching exploits, the balcony of the second church was bulging, especially on Sunday nights and during the week. Over 2,000 converts were attending regularly but again, as in the first church, the problem was where to seat them.

Cameras were bought and installed outside the main sanctuary, allowing the overflow of people to watch services live on television. The hallway of the church was also used as a seating area and a big screen was erected in a corner.

Inside, people were standing in the aisles as the local revival continued to spread.

The immense growth in the second house brought forth another chapter in the remarkable life of Pastor James McConnell. Realising something had to be done to accommodate these souls, he began to search for a piece of land again.

Although his flock didn't know it at the time, their pastor was attempting to build an even larger church.

Close friends of the pastor questioned the validity of this idea. As he searched relentlessly for land, some urged caution.

"What happens if your popularity wanes? You will be left with a big white elephant," they insisted.

James, however, was still confident because he believed that it was not so much that he was popular, but rather that the Spirit of God was in his church.

It was while walking by a field on the Shore Road in Belfast one afternoon that the pastor felt the presence of God come upon him.

He could see in it the potential to build a massive house for the Lord. Back in 1963, God had told him that one day he would use James to build a huge sanctuary in North Belfast. Some believed that the current church at the time on the Whitewell Road was the fulfilment of that particular   vision, but James always knew in his heart that there was another project still to complete.

He enquired about the price of the land which he understood would cost a fortune to acquire. Immediately he offered £150,000 for it, but learned that there was a business concern in England expressing an interest. They confirmed this by offering £200,000. Eventually bidding reached £450,000 and the pastor said he would match that.

Suddenly, however, the English company withdrew from the bidding and the land became the property of the Whitewell Church. It was at this point that Pastor McConnell showed his understanding of business affairs. His apparent lack of interest meant that the land was secured for just £230,000 - a saving of £220,000.

Plans were drawn up and the Whitewell people informed about the venture. Eventually a model of the magnificent new church - which was estimated to cost around £3.5 million - was designed and shown to the Whitewell congregation. The pastor, along with Belfast architect Barry Patterson, then travelled to Texas to study the design of one of the largest Full Gospel churches there.

Although not a carbon copy, it was hoped that the new church would be similar to some in the United States. Describing its appeal to his faithful congregation was a dream for the pastor.

"It is really mind-blowing," he told them one evening, following his return from the USA. "An octagonal shape with the pulpit at the front and a sloping floor to the gallery. It rises towards a central lantern light and ventilation and there will be two entrances. The stained-glass windows from the existing church will be used, but in a more imaginative way, and the small hall will have the possibility of bookshops, various pastoral rooms and counselling rooms with television monitors," added the pastor.

As building work commenced, motorists using one of Belfast's main motorways, the M2, witnessed the new Tabernacle literally rise from the ground. Its huge structure, outlined in iron girders, gradually took on a more definite shape as the bricks and mortar were added.

The splendid internal features were, of course, hidden from the public gaze at this stage, as was the identity of one of the moving forces behind the superb building - Harland and Wolff. How fitting that it should be the Belfast shipbuilders who would ensure a superb finish when one considers that James had been their employee many years before.

Having completed work on other projects like the Foyle Bridge in Londonderry and the replacing of a roof at Crusaders football ground, the Metropolitan contract was a job the Yard were pleased to get.

Certainly James's former company was responsible for most of the high quality work at the Tabernacle - the pulpit, stairways and such like. They were employed to make all the heavy wooden doors and door frames for the church and fitted thousands of metres of ash skirting. Much of the wrought iron and brass work was also undertaken by their skilled workers.

As people came to see the fantastic progress of the church, many were overwhelmed and burst into tears, such was the effect upon them.

Men, women and children worked together in harmony, but there was still a very important question left unanswered. How would the pastor raise £3.5 million in just three years?

That estimated cost rose to around £5 million and the pastor was aware of the Lord's principle that debt was not acceptable. Naturally he wanted to make sure that when the doors of the new building officially opened most of the costs would already be accounted for.

The burden increased upon the pastor, who collected an amazing figure of £125,000 during a special offering at the church. That cash helped launch the building fund and pay for the piling at the site. Before long workmen were hired and many other gift days helped to pay their wages. But considering James was a pastor and not a businessman by profession, it was clear that he would have to seek good advice on many aspects of the building project. He had no yardstick to go by as one of the last men to attempt a similar undertaking was Spurgeon, back in the nineteenth century.

The pastor's business acumen and wisdom increased, however, as did his confidence at the way the site was developing. He informed the workmen not to do deals without his permission and James believed God had told him to handle the financial side of the construction. He began to realise that if you have cash it is amazing what you can achieve and, determined to stick to his budget, he got certain materials for almost nothing.

He was also extremely judicious when it came to the handling of large sums of money. Two years before he considered building the Tabernacle, James led to Christ an old friend who was a financial advisor. The new convert was able to give the pastor regular counsel about how to handle the huge offerings he was now receiving. Remarkably, inside five years James had made a profit of £1 million due to some sound investments. If you consider that the Whitewell church was also now committed to donating over £100,000 each year to foreign missions, that achievement is all the more amazing.

The bank managers were astonished at the shrewdness James displayed. One financial consultant even commented that the pastor was in the wrong job, but through it all, he was obviously seeing the wisdom of God in a man.

Like the late 1970's, armchair critics were quick to react about how much money was being sunk into the Metropolitan project. They slated the scheme as nothing more than an ego trip. Again the bulk of the criticism came from other churches, who complained that the project was too expensive and that the money raised should have been given to the poor. When the pastor heard of this he remembered Judas Iscariot in the house at Bethany.

Judas accused Mary of wasting money when she anointed Jesus with oil. Judas asked, "Why was this fragrant oil not sold for 300 pence and given to the poor?" To which Jesus replied, "Let her alone, she has kept this for my burial: For the poor you have with you always, but me you do not have always." John 12:5.

If the pastor and his people had learned anything over the years it was that to reach the poor, or anyone else, you have to find Jesus first.

With Ulster being plunged into an even darker abyss, the need for a modern-day complex to cater for the needs of broken people was James McConnell's greatest priority. He and his congregation had already proven to be a most giving church in every sphere, having donated thousands of pounds to overseas missions and to other churches in various countries. In his own words, "We had nothing to prove."

As all other financial obligations were being met, the cost of the construction increased and it is a tribute to the Lord Jesus Christ and Him alone that inside those three years over £4m was raised. Even another recession at the beginning of 1990, which affected every form of industry, failed to dampen their spirits.

Actually, the original estimate of £3.5m climbed to £7m by the official opening, but despite this the congregation managed to raise the funds. The incredible feat will be remembered most for its staggering gift day services, particularly a record collection then of £116,000 handed in at a single Lord's day service. The yearly offerings for the year 1993 were also well over £1 million.

Those working-class people put on their dungarees, picked up their tools and worked for little or no reward.

Again those early words of prophecy spring to mind, "Many visitors shall come to you by aeroplane and ship to see what the Lord has accomplished among you."

The pastor turned down a number of invitations to earn money from preaching engagements. Numerous established churches in Canada and the USA invited him, but his reason for staying again proved in hindsight to be a wise one. Afraid that the size of the offerings would drop if he left the church for a while, he believed that preaching abroad could prove counter-productive and so the pastor decided to stay in Belfast. It was a decision that certainly paid off as the needed cash poured in from his own flock.

Also developing at a phenomenal rate at this time was the income the pastor was deriving from the sale of his sermons which were being sold by cassette tape each week and sent throughout the world.

But as the pastor stuck rigidly to his policy of preaching the gospel rather than expressing his views on politics, he found himself busier than ever. Indeed such was his reputation that judges, lawyers, policemen, IRA members and terrorists from both communities came to hear what he had to say.

One evening stands out above the rest. It was a Sunday service and about 13 police landrovers surrounded the church. The pastor thought there was going to be an assassination attempt on someone, but he then discovered that the fuss was caused due to the arrival of one of the province's top judges. After the man was seated, he said to one of the faithful members: "Tell me about this preacher."

The Whitewell member replied, "He preaches Christ and Him crucified, nothing else."

By the end of the service the judge went out of the meeting born again, having committed his life to Christ.

Despite the intervening years, the pastor's main contractor John McCallister was still with him. He was responsible for the entire Tabernacle project and along with another committed and talented man, Mervyn Foster, they managed to complete the enormous construction work. Things didn't always go according to plan, but the fellowship between the workmen was wonderful.

John as foreman had to take steps to curb the pastor's enthusiasm as he was involved in everything. One day the pastor asked if he could help paint in the men's toilets. John agreed, but after 15 minutes a dear old saint who was working there, John Patterson, came out and asked if someone would drive the pastor home to prepare for the evening service.

When foreman John enquired why, brother Patterson said, "Painting is not one of James's gifts. While I have been painting the window frames, the pastor has been painting the windows."

James was eventually persuaded to go home and work on his own ministry of preaching which, of course, by God's grace, had contributed to the success of the Metropolitan Church.

As Scripture says, "Prophecy is to be judged," and if it comes to pass then it is of the Lord. That first prophecy back in the Orange Hall itself was about to be fulfilled in a most spectacular way. Months and years of difficulties had been endured for the sake of the cross. Even before the spiritual explosion within the Metropolitan Tabernacle, the Spirit had come and formed Whitewell into the reaping church that had been predicted. Actually, having taken the gospel to every town and city across the province, the Metropolitan Tabernacle was about to become the largest church in the United Kingdom.

As the pastor and his people prepared to move to their third church, it was with the knowledge that God was with them.

From a basic little hall, 37 years beforehand, the Whitewell people would now have a building which seated over 4,000 people, with an extra 1,500 catered for by way of a minor hall. Add to this a comprehensive administration department, cafeteria and an array of rooms for special functions, and few could argue that the Metropolitan Tabernacle was not a remarkable achievement which would rank with that of Charles Spurgeon who built the London Metropolitan Tabernacle.

The official opening of the Metropolitan Tabernacle, Belfast, was scheduled for Saturday, 19th February, 1994, a date the hard-working brethren made sure they kept.

As the Lord provided a burnt offering for Abraham, so too God provided whatsoever the pastor needed. That providence also extended to the necessary manpower, as key brothers and sisters joined the church and added their services to those whom Pastor McConnell refers to as "the old hands."

The new facilities were beyond the wildest dreams of the man who started the Whitewell Church back in 1957. Back then the dream was simply to create 'a light for God in a dark land, a sign of hope for the hopeless'.

By the hand of God, that dream had now become a most remarkable reality.

Chapter Twenty-One

A Day To Remember

❖

In the midst of the new £7m building that would have rivalled any hotel or entertainment complex, the opening attendance at the Whitewell Metropolitan Tabernacle was a testament to a present-day miracle.

That Saturday afternoon in February, they came in their thousands from all over the world to hear Pastor James McConnell preach from his new pulpit.

As the tape was cut at the entrance, he could not fail to compare the plush interior and the thousands gathered around him with the memories of the humble beginnings in a draughty Orange Hall. He told the crowd, "With overflowing hearts we are delighted to see you, no matter where you are from. Who would have believed that 10 people who met in an old hall on the Whitewell Road 37 years ago would be enabled under God to build such a House. This House will be for all classes, for all political persuasions. I'm delighted to see you."

Vehicle registrations from all over Northern Ireland, as well as distinctive Eire number plates, peppered the car park. The

Shore Road was congested for a quarter of a mile on either side of the Tabernacle as heavy traffic was diverted off the motorway.

As the doors opened, worshippers poured into the main auditorium. Two flights of stairs took them past walls covered in murals depicting scenes from the Bible, which reflected from a gold ceiling. A large chandelier hanging over the sanctuary competed with the daylight spilling through the stained-glass windows bearing Biblical quotations.

Parents of the children were able to leave them safely in the creche, which operated on both sides of the church. State of the art lighting and sound ensured that none of the congregation would miss anything.

Caterers had their own minor miracle to work by feeding the five thousand, as they struggled to dispense tea and sandwiches in the new church restaurant.

One family drove from as far away as Galway to witness the sight of a 150-strong choir decked in green and white robes and suits. It puts things in perspective when you consider that, in many churches, the choir alone would constitute a sizeable congregation. (More recently, the Youth and Senior choirs have amalgamated giving them a combined membership of well over three hundred).

The women wore flowing emerald and white robes, the men wore business suits and all had the air, if not the full-blown exuberance, of an American gospel choir. They were supported by a band of musicians majoring on percussion and featuring a sound system in a league of its own.

Deacons in the foyer led people to their seats. One local newspaper recalled how they brought humour to the proceedings. "Two sets of two seats," one announced, leading the way, with a joke about how they were the best seats in the house.

The entire congregation, which numbered approximately 5,000, sat and worshipped as they waited for the afternoon service to start. Yet bald statistics about size and cost and the seating capacity for the new Tabernacle don't really convey the sheer scale of the place.

The building itself gave the feel of a massive concert hall with the ground floor sloping down in tiers of theatre-style seating towards the stage. The great crescent-shaped gallery was a spectacular first glimpse for the congregation as was the light which reflected from the giant chandeliers.

At around 2:30 pm Pastor James McConnell made his way up to the front of the Tabernacle for the very first time. At 57 years of age, this was the proudest day of his life. The congregation sang a number of choruses as he arrived, dressed in an immaculate suit, but none tugged at the heart strings of his committed brethren more than, "Yesterday was different."

Yesterday was indeed different for Pastor James McConnell.

As he sat facing the huge audience, he reflected on those early days of his life. No parents, no prospects and no future, but how God had blessed him. As he addressed the massive gathering he echoed those feelings, commenting, "We say from the depths of our hearts, like David in Psalm 115, 'Not unto us, Oh Lord, not unto us, but unto thy name give glory, for thy mercy and for thy truth's sake'."

Then great applause followed as he announced, "Today I call this new House, The Whitewell Metropolitan Tabernacle, Belfast".

The dream had come true. Yet only four of that original group of ten people were there to see the new church in all its glory. "The others are with the Lord," announced Pastor McConnell.

If the official opening itself didn't constitute a miracle, the fact that there were among the congregation ex-IRA and ex-UFF terrorists, worshipping side by side with police and prison officers, certainly did. Here was proof that when the regenerating power of the gospel of the Lord Jesus Christ enters the lives of Protestants and Catholics, all forms of hatred melt away and sectarian walls come tumbling down.

Throughout that day, over 10,000 people attended two services, but the pastor left the main preaching to his boyhood friend Robert Gass, and to Rev. Wynn Lewis, Superintendent of the Elim Church. Robert Gass, like many others, had travelled from the United States to attend what the pastor still calls, "a day to remember". Making that day even more complete for him was the fact that his two great friends John and Dale Estlinbaum flew in from Houston, Texas, to help officially open the building. Dale and John have become great friends of Pastor McConnell. Indeed he has flown to Texas to visit them no fewer than 70 times during his ministry.

Pastor McConnell's greatest satisfaction, however, came not from the festivities, but from the news that a total of fifteen people were won for Christ. That gave him more pleasure than anything else and he was assured that God had stamped his seal of approval on the new building.

Chapter Twenty-Two

A Night To Remember

❖

The most outstanding event that marked the lives of James McConnell and his wife, Margaret, however, was the celebration of the pastor's 40th year in the ministry.

The date was 19th February, 1995, the venue was the Europa Hotel in Belfast. Guests from all over the world were flown across to enjoy a night of wonderful fellowship. The planning involved in this function was considerable as it was proposed to interview James in a manner similar to the television programme "This is Your Life". It was the worst-kept secret in Belfast at the time, although the pastor is adamant that he knew nothing about it.

"That was a wonderful night, especially to see so many old friends from all over the world. I couldn't have dreamed of such an evening. It is one I will never forget," he recalls.

There were many tributes paid to James that night by his pastors, friends and family. Rumour has it that he is still trying to finish off the huge cake that was baked by one of his congregation!

The evening began with announcements and the reading of telegrams from churches across the world. But when James was handed the 'big red book,' and told, "James McConnell, this is your life," the place completely erupted in applause.

Never a man to be taken by surprise, the Belfast pastor on this occasion was rendered speechless and the church's musicians added an authentic touch to the evening by pre-recording the music from the TV programme.

As he and his wife Margaret walked to their seats, the many guests and well-wishers stood and applauded the pastor.

When Margaret was called upon to speak, she said, "Sometimes my husband's love for pets has left me confused, especially when he arrives home from his pastoral duties. One day I heard the front door opening and James shouted, 'Are you there, wee love?'

"I replied, 'Yes,' but soon realised James was talking to one of the cats and not to me!"

It was a memorable moment that brought the house down, one that the pastor's congregation would forever treasure.

Erected on the stage was a large screen, which the interviewer used to show old photographs of James during his youth. Many guests from the USA, Canada, Spain and many parts of the British Isles, had been secretly lined up to attend.

As they came up to the front to pay tribute to James, it was clear that all of them had one thing in common - a real love for Jesus Christ and for the pastor who had led many of them to Christ. Many of those attending had been saved under his ministry.

Present were his entire church staff, pastors who had been with him for years, others who had joined in along the way. His good friends, Americans John and Dale Estlinbaum, were again with him, but stealing the show for the pastor was the entrance of his young granddaughter, Rebecca. She came on at the end, making it all a memorable night for the pastor and his family.

That evening gave him the opportunity to reflect on forty years in the service of God.

It was during this period that the pastor and his family moved from their original home at Serpentine Road, which was situated in a Nationalist area. He had been there for 28 years, but prior to the opening of the Tabernacle his wife and family were constantly being harassed by Nationalist youths, who also broke many windows at his home. They were also robbed on a number of occasions and the incidents became so frequent that he even stopped reporting it to the police. Instead, he considered the prospect of relocating and finally did so at Greenisland, about four miles from the Tabernacle.

He laughs at exaggerated gossip, which suggested he moved to a palace. His house is, in fact, a modest bungalow. Stories about him abound. He's accused of owning a ranch somewhere on the coast, and having amassed a personal fortune. Opinion is divided on whether his personal aircraft is a jet or a helicopter and the story is that you can recognise it parked at Aldergrove Airport because it's painted in the same colours as the Whitewell buses!

It is all nonsense. James McConnell didn't even have a personal bank account until 1995 when the church held a reception for the pastor and his wife and presented them with one.

In no way is the house like Buckingham Palace as is constantly reported. The new property has just three bedrooms, a small study, a living room and dining room. If there is a luxury for James it is the addition of a good sized garden, something he didn't have, of course, back in those early days in Spring Street.

Other accusations which have dogged him over the years surround his theology. He is accused of not believing in the Trinity, but naturally that's an accusation he treats more seriously and continues to deny strenuously. The fact that the church is affiliated with the Elim Church proves, he says, that he does believe in the Trinity, as he could not have that relationship with that particular movement if he was unsound in this doctrine.

He has taken so much criticism over the years that it is beginning to take its toll on him. He's fed up with it. He seems to get more criticism from people who profess to know Christ than those who do not. "This is disappointing, if not disgraceful," he says.

Some drive past in big cars and criticise everything that is going on in the Tabernacle, such as the services, the singing, the cost and high standard of the church. But the pastor is quick to point out how these same people are living in big houses in rich areas of Northern Ireland and have absolutely no contact with ordinary working people. He has walked the streets and knocked every door in the area, ten times over.

Pastor McConnell feels he and his church are meeting the needs of people from every background.

Chapter Twenty-Three

Day By Day

❖

The Metropolitan Tabernacle, Belfast, is more than just a place of worship - it is a centre of spiritual teaching and non-stop Christ-centred activities.

Most of the members who belonged to the first and second church were working-class people who lived right on its doorstep. Times have changed and the membership today is made up of different classes arriving from all parts of Northern Ireland.

Converts are drawn initially because of the great Christian oratory, but on arrival at the Tabernacle they soon realise that there is more to the place than the preacher and his pulpit.

Due to Pastor McConnell's organisational and administrative skills, combined with his dedicated staff, the Tabernacle has managed to establish ten Sunday Schools throughout Ulster, ten churches at home and abroad and 'Bus Outreach' which now sends transport to over 30 different locations around the countryside.

In addition there is the cassette tape ministry, a magazine and literature department, a youth club and youth centre, young converts' class, choirs and orchestra, a senior citizens' group, tract distribution, Girls' Brigade and Boy Scouts, a full-time staff and foreign missionaries.

Powerful prayer meetings, the prophetic word, and rapid growth in the largest full gospel church in the British Isles are reasons why this centre of worship is truly the work of the Lord. Indeed the Tabernacle is often referred to as a veritable beehive of holy activity.

The Tabernacle is a place of incessant activity from 7:30 am each morning to 10:30 pm at night. But despite the growth of the church and its outreach, the pastor gains most satisfaction from the large increase at the weekly prayer meetings and the Bible study. For him it is a dream come true as he recollects how, many years before, he sat in front of the fire on a Saturday night in the early sixties and read about the phenomenal growth of Willie Mullan's Bible Class. He never could have visualised then that he would double that achievement.

Our current generation is like the Laodicean church mentioned in Revelation, neither cold nor hot: but lukewarm in its approach. John, speaking about the end times, says in Revelation 3:15,16, "I know thy works, that thou art neither cold nor hot: I would thou wert cold or hot. So then because thou art lukewarm and neither cold nor hot, I will spue thee out of my mouth."

Few Bible scholars disagree that many churches today are the very kind that John was referring to. The great affluence and extreme materialism which currently prevails in many parts of Europe has seen a massive decline in church attendances throughout the entire Western World, certainly during the last quarter of a century.

Why, then, in an era which is considered to be the 'last days', and when church attendance is falling, are thousands coming out to the Metropolitan Tabernacle? Many have asked such a question on hearing that no fewer than five thousand people go in and out of the Tabernacle doors every Sunday. The pastor's answer is simple. "I am not any different to other servants of God in this land. There are many sincere Christians who love the Lord Jesus Christ as much as I do and, in fact, possibly love Him more, but God has blessed this work and only He knows why."

Despite the large attendances at the Tabernacle, however, few need to stand outside it, as was the case in the old days. The increase in numbers has been substantial since 1994. Attendance at the Breaking of Bread services has risen by approximately seven hundred people compared with the second church on the Whitewell Road. But, significantly, the congregation has doubled on Sunday evenings from 1,500 in the old church to just over 3,000 - a phenomenon by modern-day standards.

To supervise such an influx of new converts is demanding, to say the least, but a glance at the pastor's rigorous schedule gives one an idea of his tremendous commitment.

For example, he begins each day at 7:30 am and remains at the Tabernacle for about an hour. Then he and Pastor Blake visit different hospitals to encourage the sick of his assembly. This has been his practice every day since starting the Whitewell Church in 1957. They return for the end of the morning prayer meeting which takes place five days each week from 9 am to 10 am. The pastor spends another hour attending to business matters and then goes off to do his own calls which take up the rest of the morning.

After lunch, he starts writing sermons for his three main addresses that week. In addition to this, he is on duty at the Monday and Friday evening prayer meeting and the Wednesday night Bible Study, but such is his desire to preach that he often accepts invitations to speak at various missions on Tuesday and Thursday evenings, leaving him only Saturday night to rest.

One unsung hero, however, is the pastor's daughter Linda, who virtually single-handedly runs the entire administrative side of the church.

Linda is responsible for all documentation in relation to weddings and with such a large percentage of young people in the church this can be a sizeable task. She also acts as personal assistant to her Dad, and is accountable for the financial side of the church, ie. the paying of salaries and bills.

With her high level of competence, many members believe the pastor's daughter would rate alongside any top modern-day executive in the business sector, especially in relation to organisational skills.

She accepts, however, that one of her greatest difficulties is in the handling of requests for money. People automatically think because Whitewell is a huge church that they have money to burn, but it doesn't work like that. That's not to say the church won't help different causes and charities, but it can be difficult when separating one from the other. No Christian organisation likes to say no, but sometimes the Tabernacle just can't afford to say yes.

Thankfully Linda is supported by two other able girls, Geraldine Higgins and Sharon Perry. Geraldine, wife of Youth Pastor Shaw Higgins, is a receptionist, but helps out with many other important duties such as opening of mail, and responding to the increased demand for audio tapes and videos. Geraldine also makes out a weekly rota for the pastor, though the schedule changes frequently due to bereavements and unexpected calls. Meanwhile Sharon, who is Captain of the Girls' Brigade, is never far away in terms of lending a hand. She is a caring girl, who visits the sick and advises young people with problems. Both girls are also involved with the public, answering phones, and dealing with multiple requests for concert tickets and times of services.

But it's not just in the department of administration where there is a great need. Naturally the task of cleaning the Tabernacle is a massive one, too. It is carried out by two full-time caretakers: Norman Graham and Tommy Braden. Tommy lives on the premises and is affectionately known to the Whitewell people as, "Captain Braden." In addition to that, however, the pastor relies on what he describes as, "A wonderful band of men and women," who come to the Tabernacle every day on a voluntary basis. At least ten people can be counted upon to clean the church, and if one considers the sheer size of the property, these volunteers are of considerable help to the pastor.

The real cleaning, however, has been done in the spiritual sense, says Pastor McConnell who, like his flock, has witnessed hundreds of people asking to be washed in the blood of Jesus and cleansed from all their sins. Often he has been criticised about the type of people who have been allowed to worship in this church, but he believes men are like fish, you catch them first and then you clean them.

The most rewarding day for 'catching fish', as the pastor puts it, is on the Lord's day where both services are devoted to the winning of souls. On Sundays, too, scores of members rush home after morning worship to teach in the Sunday Schools. With an upsurge in violence, alcohol and drugs in our generation, the pastor sees this as a vital part of his ministry.

Supervisor of the Sunday School is Alec Brown, a faithful member of the Tabernacle, who for many years has been involved in this facet of the church. The Sunday School ministry, which started out in a small way, has developed into a big operation as many young families have joined the Tabernacle from various parts of Northern Ireland; and that's a development with which the pastor is delighted.

There are also a number of other ministries which operate with the blessing of the pastor and his church - the emphasis here is on outreach which may account for the rapid growth of the congregation.

The names of some of those now involved in the life of the church were once better known to the police than to the pastors. Billy Elliot was a Brigadier in the UDA in East Belfast until he was saved in 1991. Now he's responsible for organising the annual Evangelistic Tent Mission in Mersey Street, opposite the Oval, home of Glentoran Football Club - and he is training to become a full-time pastor. The fact that the mission received little or no publicity in 1996 didn't deter over six thousand people turning up for the week-long event. Indeed, during the past four years over 22,000 people have heard the gospel in that tent, resulting in the establishment of a thriving Sunday School.

But staging a mission like this is no small task as can be gauged by the amount of organising which goes into it. Pastor McConnell is not really involved in the build-up although he preaches at the meetings each evening. Instead, he leaves his colleague and friend, Billy Elliot, to handle the necessary preparations.

The mission was started in 1992, just after the former paramilitary gave his life to Christ. "I wanted the people of East Belfast to visit the new Tabernacle, but realised that wasn't always possible. So I decided if they couldn't come to us, we would bring the gospel to them," says Billy.

Each year since then he has distributed around 30,000 leaf-lets to every home in East Belfast and, along with a group of fellow believers, has laboured faithfully in what, after all, used to be his old stomping ground. Then there has been the erecting of the tent, which is large enough to hold 1,200 people. Approximately fifty or sixty men and women are on hand to help, while security is also arranged to look after the tent 24 hours a day during the course of the week. A caravan parked in the field close by is also guarded by volunteers.

Buses are then sent from the Tabernacle to every location in greater Belfast and it's the sight of 400 cars and thirty buses parked beside the tent each night which makes this 'tent mission' that little bit different.

Another key conversion at the Metropolitan Tabernacle has been Hugh Lamont. "Bootsie," as he is affectionately nicknamed by the congregation, stunned the local police when he gave his life to Christ in 1994. A former alcoholic and drug addict, Hugh now leads a team of evangelists which operates in Belfast's Golden Mile. They start at 11:00 pm and work throughout the night, witnessing to the girls working the streets, to drug addicts and to alcoholics.

This is difficult and often dangerous work, but the team is sustained by love for their Saviour. When they return from the streets tired and sometimes discouraged they remember the words of Christ, "Because ye have done it unto the least of one of these my brethren, ye did it unto Me."

The Tabernacle also organises no fewer than five open-air gospel meetings each week. Rain, hail or shine, these meetings are held in Lisburn, Glengormley, Belfast's Shankill Road, Carrickfergus and Rathcoole. All are a vital part of Whitewell's weekly witness.

In all this endeavour, James has been enabled under God to accomplish a quite remarkable ministry.

"It is not man's doing, but God's," said one particular visitor to the Tabernacle, after he called during the hub of a normal day. The man, a professing Catholic, added:

"I go to my church during the day for peace and quiet, but the Tabernacle is such a contrast in that it is full of daily activity. In one room I found a prayer group, in another there was a children's creche. Then there was a healing class and others were setting up sound equipment for the evening service. Some were having tea and coffee in the restaurant, others were involved in the Youth Centre, playing snooker, badminton and keeping fit. There were pastors counselling and a man sitting on the stage of the main auditorium singing to the Lord. Others were cleaning and singing as they worked. Despite all these activities, I was still conscious of a presence I had never felt before. Even with all the noise, I had found the peace I was looking for and I'm sure it was the very presence of God."

This person, like many others who visit the Tabernacle, had uncovered a great truth, namely, that the people of the Metropolitan Tabernacle adore their Saviour Jesus Christ. Their lives revolve around the Lord's work at the Tabernacle.

Like David, these worshippers can say, "In thy presence is fullness of joy; at thy right hand there are pleasures for evermore." Psalm 16:11.

Chapter Twenty Four

IF THE LORD WILLS

❖

In addition to all this, Pastor McConnell still intends to build a retirement home for his older members, directly beside the Tabernacle.

The young people have received so much over the past few years that he doesn't want the elderly to think they have been forgotten. His aim is to ensure that they will be well looked after.

There are already two young men who have dedicated themselves to visiting the elderly during the evenings, while seven other full-time pastors at the Tabernacle keep in touch during the day.

Some may comment that it is the job of the state to look after pensioners, but the pastor believes it is his responsibility to look after the needs of those who have been faithful members of the Whitewell Church over the years.

The new retirement home will mean that these people will only have a short distance to walk to their weekly services of worship and, of course, if some of these converts are ill it will be much easier to visit them and keep a caring watch over them.

He stresses, however, that should this be accomplished it will not be the end of his overall vision for the Metropolitan Tabernacle. He still expects to engage in one of the greatest challenges of his life - the building of an aids clinic, again, adjacent to the church. This is by far the greatest ambition before he retires and he is already investigating such a possibility. This may seem pie-in-the-sky at present, but given his track record over the years in carrying out that which God has commanded him to do, it is surely not beyond the realms of possibility.

Recently it seems that the aids virus has been played down in our country and in the United Kingdom, but the multitude of people who have contracted this disease has brought to Pastor McConnell's attention the need for not just an aids clinic, but a rehabilitation centre for drug and alcohol-related problems, too.

He is absolutely serious about this venture.

"If I am going to do it, I will do it right. It won't be a half-hearted effort. It will be a professional and top-class involvement and no money will be spared," he promises.

The pastor wants to take care of these sick and wounded individuals, but he also believes that they need to accept Christ if they are to make a genuine and lasting transformation in their lives. For him, the key in that transformation is in proper Christian counselling and in the love of God.

Pastor McConnell concedes he has much to accomplish before the end of his ministry and his desire to erect a centre for the elderly and an aids clinic is commendable, given what has already been achieved at the Tabernacle. Another ambition, however, is to begin his own Bible School at the new Tabernacle. The class would consist mainly of young students who, he hopes, would come from different parts of the globe.

The idea originated after a number of ministers in the United States attended the Tabernacle for two weeks to see how such a huge church functioned. Their conclusion was that hundreds of other ministers, particularly young pastors, needed to experience for themselves how the Tabernacle operated on a daily basis. One minister even offered to send 20 students to be schooled by Pastor McConnell, convinced that they would return with a different perspective on church life. Lack of time unfortunately meant that such an invitation had to be declined.

Having said this, the pastor wants his own Bible School up and running before he retires, but like the expansion of the tape ministry he is exercising caution before taking that step. He is looking for the right men to teach in this school but feels that there is a great dearth of quality around. He knows he could employ teachers at any time, but he is looking for experienced men ... men who don't just show you how to run a church, preach and minister, but men who tell you why it's done that way.

He makes the point that Elijah and Elisha both had Bible schools but, significantly, it was they who presided over them.

He cites Spurgeon's Bible school as a yardstick - and an example of the kind of man he's looking for. Every Friday morning Spurgeon's students looked forward to the 'governor' coming to lecture. They were excited because they knew that God was using Spurgeon in a wonderful way and that he was well qualified to instruct any aspiring preacher.

The pastor loves the tale about the young man who arrived at Spurgeon's Bible class one day and asked, "Sir, why is it that you are winning souls every week and I am not?"

Spurgeon replied, "Do you mean to tell me that every time you preach the gospel, you expect souls to be saved?"

"Oh, no, not at all," said the young student.

"Then that is exactly why you don't get any!" added Spurgeon.

Perhaps it is too much to hope for a Spurgeon, or a Wesley, an Elijah or Elisha, but whoever James finds, he is convinced that he will not get any more than one or two good men to teach in his school. "History dictates that," he insists, adding, "There were fifty sons of the prophets, but they just faded from the picture. On the other hand, Elisha was with Elijah for just ten years, yet how wonderfully God anointed him."

Any thoughts of the pastor and his flock taking a back seat, having moved to the comfortable surroundings of the new Tabernacle, haven't materialised at all. On the contrary, since arriving at the Shore Road Church, prolonged periods of prayer have been undertaken. This was always the practice at the other churches.

Both these projects for old people and for those suffering from the aids virus may take another five to ten years to complete, but to finish out his ministry with these in place would fulfil for him the vision God has given him for his life.

The Tabernacle supports a number of foreign missions as well. Missionaries have left for Spain, China and other countries, and large amounts of cash are sent to Eastern Europe. This money is gathered by weekly collections outside the Tabernacle on behalf of the latest world crisis. Bosnia, Africa and many third-world countries benefit from these gifts. The entire operation centres around the role of the pastor who has been the instigator of this work.

Pastor McConnell always keeps a tight rein on the financial affairs and when money is required for any particular cause, his staff reply:

"You'll have to see the 'Bishop.'"

Only those who know him intimately call him by this title, but it's common knowledge to the majority of his congregation.

He still resists the temptation to employ people in a full-time capacity, in case the rush for tapes amounts only to what he calls, "a time of blessing.' In his heart, though, he believes that full-time staff will become inevitable and that a whole department dedicated to the publishing industry could well be necessary before the turn of the century.

Many of his congregation have also urged the pastor to produce a monthly magazine - one that will allow him to express his views on the church and other topical issues. His flock believe that, due to the sheer size of the Tabernacle and its growing list of activities, such a newsletter would be of considerable help to local and international members, keeping them informed of life at Whitewell. That is something he is contemplating, sooner rather than later, but as always he takes his lead from the Holy Spirit, who has the final say on what he can and cannot do.

One of the pastor's greatest attributes is his ability to make decisions when the time is right. Even though he accepts that he is impetuous by nature, he is rarely coerced to do anything before being instructed by the Holy Spirit. This gift has helped him select the right people for the right posts and has prevented him from making costly errors in his Christian ministry. Moreover, it is perhaps the biggest single reason why he has been used in a mighty way by the Lord Jesus Christ. He has always sought the will of God in every aspect of his life; hence, God has been able to use him.

As the Tabernacle grows at an unprecedented rate, the pastor is keen to emphasise that despite its popularity he has no intentions of starting his own movement. He is content being affiliated to the Elim Church and is more concerned with winning souls for Christ than people for himself.

Chapter Twenty Five

THE WORLD HIS PARISH

❖

The year 1996 produced another significant development in the progress of the Metropolitan Tabernacle - the explosion of what is known as the tape ministry.

Although this ministry has been in operation since the 1970s, it has only really taken off in recent years. The ordering of weekly tapes and sermons has trebled since the official opening of the new Tabernacle.

The idea behind the ministry is to tell the world the great truth about the gospel and to help change the lives of people who live without Christ.

This objective has already been realised in dramatic fashion. The Whitewell Church has received hundreds of letters of testimony from people in the United Kingdom and further afield.

Tapes of the pastor's sermons have been sent to countries like New Zealand, Australia, Canada, Sweden, United States, and Nigeria, and in every case word has returned to the Tabernacle that souls have been saved through this ministry.

How true the scripture, "Cast thy bread upon the waters for thou shalt find it after many days." Eccles. 11:1.

Such an international demand for his sermons is because of the continual preaching of the gospel, as well as the considerable blessing of God. He has, of course, always ensured that his sermons major on the work of the cross. In the words of the hymn writer they simply, but powerfully, tell 'the old, old story of Jesus and his love.' "Men and women are saved by grace, and grace alone," he says. Biblical words like 'saved' and 'lost' are often part of his message and words like 'heaven' and 'hell' are a vital component in what he terms his old-fashioned gospel message.

James has always viewed his work seriously, believing that his life has been shaped in the broad current of God's will, and the rise of the tape ministry is just another confirmation of this. Like the Wesleys and Spurgeons of this world, he has begun a task as challenging as that of any man - and if the world is to become his parish it would require the blessings of heaven upon his work.

The pastor's tapes are broadcast all over the world these days, particularly in the USA.

It is, nevertheless, a considerable undertaking to run an operation like the tape ministry on a part-time basis. In this respect the pastor is fortunate to have the services of Jim Thompson, who has been involved in it for many years. His day starts at 7.30 am and ends around lunch-time, but it is quite a commitment as he works seven days each week and is often required on many other occasions. Many nights are spent burning the midnight oil in the tape room with other Christian helpers.

Jim has come a long way from the days when the tape ministry began. Back then he used to make around one hundred tapes each week in his spare time and give them away to those who needed spiritual help. Today, literally thousands of tapes are sold world-wide. So busy has this department of the Tabernacle become that two other men have been added to it. Both Mervyn Foster and Millar Sempey are used as back-up should demand ever exceed supply.

Every single service is recorded and this has been the case for the past 25 years. Tapes have to be marked and filed away in a huge library, which requires considerable attention to detail. They are then put out for sale at the Monday and Wednesday meetings as well as on Sundays. There is an extra dimension, though, as Jim has to respond to the needs of those who ask for tapes in bulk. For example, it is not uncommon for groups or other churches to order hundreds of tapes for their own people.

But the most heartening thing for Pastor McConnell has been the phenomenal interest in the tape ministry from various countries and the way in which the tapes have helped certain individuals.

Without food it is impossible to survive, and spiritually speaking, it's the same with the word of God. People, whether they be in England, Scotland, or America, are crying out for the bread of life - the Bible. If they can't get it in a church, then the pastor sees no reason why they should not invest in tapes which will sustain them and ensure they get properly fed from the Word of God.

Having said that, the pastor in no way condones deliberate absence from church. He confirms the importance of church attendance by way of 1st Corinthians chapter one, which declares that the church is the fellowship of God's Son. Or, as the psalmist proclaims in Psalm 77:13, "Thy way, O God, is in the sanctuary: who is so great a God as our God?"

Experience has taught him over the years that those who don't attend church suffer spiritually. Even those who attend fairly regularly, but not consistently, fall into this bracket. He loves to quote the verse of scripture, "Not forsaking the assembling of ourselves together, as the manner of some is; but exhorting one another: and so much the more, as ye see the day approaching." Hebrews 10: 25.

Although not directly related to the tape ministry, there was an incident that occurred in the Tabernacle during 1995 which is a significant endorsement of the advantages of the 'television and video age.'

It happened during the BBC programme 'Wogan's Island,' which was broadcast in Ireland at that time. After hearing about the progress of the Belfast Tabernacle, well-known television presenter, Terry Wogan, compiled a report on Pastor McConnell.

As the programme was being screened, an unsaved man watching in Wales became intrigued by the preaching and, turning to his Christian son, he asked:

"Is that man born again?"

When the son answered "Yes," his father began to sob uncontrollably in front of the television set. Before the end of the transmission, the son had the joy of leading his dad to Christ.

The story didn't end there, however. A few weeks later, the young man wrote to Pastor McConnell to thank him for preaching the truth in such a courageous way, and to tell him that just a few hours after his dad had accepted Christ, he had suffered a heart attack and died.

It is just one of many remarkable events which have given rise to the Whitewell tape ministry.

Chapter Twenty Six

A New Generation Of Leaders

---------------------------------- ❖ ----------------------------------

S trong and successful leaders are those who continually keep their house in order, but they often have many other qualities and one of those is the ability to have a 'knock-on' effect upon others. It is known simply in today's language as motivational skills.

Pastor James McConnell is one such leader.

In recent years many young men have been influenced by the tremendous impact of the pastor's own leadership, particularly his powerful preaching. The result has been a number of other aspiring young ministers arriving on the scene at Whitewell. At present there are at least twenty young men with holy ambition, straining at the leash, hoping to emerge as part of a new generation. Most of them were saved under Pastor McConnell's ministry. They have grown up under his tutoring and have developed a great love and respect for their pastor.

The pastor says that these twenty men are the cream of his church, but also admits there are many other young converts interested in serving God on a full-time basis. Such a development has placed an extra burden upon the pastor with regard to the training of these young servants.

Interestingly, that growth was not unexpected. Upon receiving the vision to build the Tabernacle, the pastor was led by the Holy Spirit in a word of prophecy to include a special room for the training of what he calls today, "A new generation of leaders.'

Named the "Magee Room of Learning", its function is to raise a number of 'special vessels' whose own godly leadership will command the attention of thousands.

The room was dedicated to the late Gordon Magee, the pastor's personal friend and the man who helped him so much during his youth.

Perhaps even now God has chosen a new Whitefield, Wesley or Spurgeon to take over from Pastor McConnell as leader of the Metropolitan Tabernacle. Certainly Pastor McConnell hopes that is the case. Every young man with promise is a potential successor for the church, but as yet the pastor has not been given any indication from the Holy Spirit as to whom it may be.

Over the last few years this has been uppermost in his mind. He has scrutinised various young men and prayed for them continually, but the whole thing rests upon God anointing the right one. The pastor doesn't only want someone with ability, as he says there are lots of people with ability. He doesn't only want someone who can preach, either, as a lot of people can preach. He desperately requires someone with an anointing from God.

He has tried to make provision for this man and the next generation by saving money for him and organising the work. Like David, who wasn't allowed to build the house of the Lord, but still gathered the wood, the materials, the gold, the silver and the brass for his son, so too the pastor has been busy gathering on behalf of the man who is to succeed him.

Certainly the facilities and educational aids in the Magee Room are of the highest standard. Its library is full of the works of the Puritans, and there is a comprehensive range of the most widely read commentaries. The young students can use the facility on a daily basis, even staying overnight providing they are using the room for studying.

Lectures are currently held within the Magee Room. It is what is known at Whitewell as 'a ministerial meeting.' Each lecture starts around 7 pm in the evening and finishes at 11.30 pm.

Despite its appeal, however, the new study wasn't an instant hit after the move to the Tabernacle. It lay empty for a while as members of the congregation, including those aspiring preachers, took time to settle into their new church. Old habits were hard to break, as in previous years Bible studies were held in people's homes or in less extravagant surroundings than the Tabernacle. The pastor personally undertook the lecturing in those days, but after some time a man called Eric Briggs became a faithful tutor.

The pastor has always employed a strict rule when allowing entrance into additional Bible studies and in assessing whether or not certain individuals are ready for the ministry.

"Come back in five years time and if you are still keen I will accept you."

That is his message to those who enquire about God's work. He claims it is a good way to prove if the call of God is authentic in their lives. How similar the advice is to that given by Gamaliel in Acts chapter five. He told the Sanhedrin, "And now I say unto you, refrain from these men and let them alone: for if this counsel or this work be of men, it will come to nought, but if it be of God ye cannot overthrow it, lest haply ye be found even to fight against God" Acts 5:38, 39.

The pastor knows that if a young man returns after five years and is still as enthusiastic as ever about the ministry, then there is probably something within that same person's spirit which makes him suitable for a calling to God's work.

The purpose of the Bible school, however, is not to produce men with degrees or letters after their names; rather, as in the case of the other churches that have already been planted, these servants are sent forth with one purpose - to win over the souls of men.

On the subject of building churches, the pastor has generally attained success, but he has had a few disastrous experiences as well. From then on he promised the Lord that he wouldn't erect another church until God put one into his hand. Since that prayer three churches have been constructed, resulting in three more young men being employed in full-time ministry.

The pastor believes this progression will continue, particularly as he is hoping for ten more years of his own ministry, which should give him time to school these men.

As the rapid growth of the Tabernacle has become more obvious, a rumour has circulated around the confines of the pastor's church in recent years that God has given him a vision to build no fewer than one hundred new churches. But he dismisses this saying, "I never had such a vision, but what the Lord did tell me was that Whitewell would be like Joseph - a fruitful bough, even a fruitful bough by a well whose branches run over the wall."

He is endeavouring to ensure that these 'branches over the wall,' are educated with fire.

"There are lots of educated ministries in Great Britain today and, while that is commendable, there is no fire," says the pastor. He adds, "Wesley was educated, but there was a fire in his ministry. Spurgeon had a brilliant mind, but he also had fire. Henry Jowett was bright, but his fire was brighter still. If you look at the great men of God, all of them had a balance of education and fiery preaching."

It's a point he is strong on, as he is frightened that his own students will focus too much on the need for qualifications and degrees to the extent that they neglect the practical side of their ministry. He is looking for degrees in dedication, degrees in achievement, but he stresses that he also believes strongly in a formal education.

Strangely, the pastor is not overly-fussed about where his young men get that education, providing it is in a Christ-centred college. Despite his own plans to train young preachers, he says, "I would be absolutely delighted if one of my young men announced that he was studying elsewhere. After all we are the body of Christ and these other colleges are part of Christ's body ... they are part of Christ's education."

Having spent over 40 years in God's work, James now believes he can provide a great wealth of instruction and power for all men wishing to take up the ministry.

He is greatly encouraged by the emergence of some of his own pastors, especially since the opening of the new Tabernacle. He describes Pastor Michael Bunting as "One of the greatest inspirational preachers I have heard," and says of Pastor Norman Hobson, "He has one of the most comprehensive ministries for a young man that I have witnessed in over forty years of God's work."

The rest of his pastors are equally talented in their own particular fields of shepherding the flock. He adds, "You couldn't shock these men. They are brilliant pastors who are shock-proof. They have dealt with every kind of situation over the years."

His pastors have experienced what he calls, "An awful lot of dirt, but dirt that is worth digging up." He explains, "Underneath the dirt, there is sometimes a jewel, underneath the dirt there is gold, underneath the dirt there is silver, so I have no reservation about taking all the dirt that is coming to me, because today's dirt is tomorrow's gold. In other words today's vilest sinner can sometimes become tomorrow's greatest Christian."

Distinguishing who God's true servants really are is not always easy, and it's something which no amount of training within a Bible school can prepare a person for.

He says, "There have been people who have joined the church at Whitewell and I thought they would become great Christians, but they didn't make it. Then there are others who I thought would never make it, but God re-created them in His own image by the power of the Holy Spirit and inspired them and used them mightily for God's glory."

It has taken considerable faith to stand by people like that, not to mention personal sacrifice and an abundance of prayer. Pastor McConnell, however, believes in the expression, 'Let your prayers take legs,' and believes also in the principle that there are many times when we can help answer our own prayers. This is something which is top of his training agenda when it comes to advising young students.

For example, when he asked for a bigger church, God replied, 'You build it and I will meet the need.' When he asked for more members, God replied, 'You walk the streets and find them and I will save them.' When he asked God for the Tabernacle and the Magee Room of Learning, God replied, 'You build it and I will fill it.'

Such an attitude has helped Pastor McConnell to meet the needs not only of his young men, but of his entire congregation. He doesn't believe in sitting back and letting God do everything. That's not to say he is putting man's effort before God's grace; rather, like the apostle Paul says, 'he is working according to the power that worketh in him.'

He urges his young men and others who are involved with God's work not to be lazy or lacking in faith. He preaches from a practical point of view, having had a wealth of experience in this department.

To illustrate his own level of faith, he tells his young students the story of how he went to visit a member of his congregation some years ago. The woman had been quite ill and had very little money at the time. He went to make the lady some lunch, but found that she had no food in the house. The pastor had just been given what he described as a 'big white fiver' that particular day - currency which would be worth around one hundred pounds in today's money. After finding out that the lady had neither food nor money, the pastor got down on his knees and asked God to meet her need. Suddenly the Holy Spirit spoke to him and said 'I have met her need, it is in your back pocket.' Even though it was the only money he had, the pastor gave it to the woman in obedience to the will of the Holy Spirit.

The woman made a full recovery from her illness and in future years gave thousands of pounds to help in the building of the new Tabernacle. She never forgot her pastor's act of kindness all those years before and in fact on her death she left everything in her will for the work of the church. "These are the sort of practical lessons young preachers need to learn," he says.

This tuition has produced much fruit as a number of churches have requested the services of the pastor's pupils. Many ministers have telephoned him and asked for a young servant to come and speak to them, as the calibre of that young man had been apparent when preaching at open-air missions.

Churches which have experienced problems have also written to Pastor McConnell and asked for a man to help in their specific situation. New branches over the wall which have gone out across the United Kingdom are further examples of the way in which the entire ministry at Whitewell is in constant demand.

Chapter Twenty Seven

REMARKABLE GROWTH

❖

Very few people outside Pastor McConnell's own assembly are fully aware that today he is shepherd to no fewer than ten other churches around the world.

Since the 1970's, new witnesses have sprung up in Newry, Londonderry, Falkirk, Scotland, Hull, Withernsea (England), and Penywaun (Wales) not to mention four churches in operation on the Costa Brava in Spain.

It was the church in Spain which arrived first. During his early days at Whitewell, Pastor McConnell came to know a man named Leslie Lyons. The pastor was looking for a faithful person to begin a great work for the Kingdom in Spain. Even though the Holy Spirit had told him who this person was, he was waiting for confirmation.

It was no surprise to the pastor when Leslie Lyons expressed with great assurance that God had called him to this work and declared his determination to spend his life preaching the gospel and winning souls.

Few can doubt that it was of God. Leslie and his wife Brenda have served faithfully there for over twenty years.

The church in Spain was the start of what the Whitewell congregation now refer to as "The branches over the wall."

The pastors of these churches have been groomed under the leadership of Pastor McConnell and generally operate under the umbrella of the Whitewell ministry. These men were so moved by the spiritual zeal of Pastor McConnell that nothing else would suffice in their lives but the preaching of the gospel.

All were and still are on fire for God, but significantly the pastor says, "All were called of God, too. You can have all the fire in the world, but if you are not called to your ministry you will never succeed."

Certainly the progress of these churches has been impressive. George McKimm arrived to pastor a congregation of 50 people at Falkirk in 1986, but today has over 300 converts. Terry Fettis has served faithfully for nine years in Londonderry, David Purse in Withernsea and John Thompson in Hull have been used tremendously by God - and the most recent pastor to go into full-time ministry is Timothy Bailie in Newry. The church in Wales is being looked after by a man called Billy Stewart, until, as the pastor puts it, "God's man comes along."

Notwithstanding the fact that Pastor McConnell had experienced great blessings in those other churches, business has continued as usual in the magnificent new Tabernacle. His ministry has since reached heights that it never attained before.

Instead of an average of eight decisions for Christ, which the pastor used to get regularly in the second church each Sunday evening, that figure today is around twenty-five.

Church statistics reveal that, in the first two years, more than two and a half thousand people have been won for Christ in the opulent surroundings of the new Tabernacle. A tally like this was a powerful way to answer the critics, who said that such a grand place couldn't possibly have the spirit of God within it.

Yet with the move came a significant change, not only in the ministry of Pastor McConnell, but in the man himself. The great animation James exhibited during his younger days has gradually been superseded by a more mature delivery in his preaching. By his own admission, he is older and hasn't the same energy as before and he is counting on the Holy Ghost more than ever.

He also admits that in the old days there was a lot of what he calls, "Perspiration mixed with inspiration."

Today he leans totally on the Lord Jesus Christ. Indeed, the huge numbers coming to Christ in the Tabernacle may well be a reflection of that new-found dependence on his Saviour. The Lord has settled his heart. He knows he has God's blessing to carry God's vision through, not looking to the left or to the right.

As the church has increased in stature over the years, the health of James McConnell has declined, affecting his physical condition somewhat. He frequently suffers from bouts of coughing which are so bad he struggles to preach. It has been the one single impediment during his ministry; a throw-back, he believes, to his days in Spring Street, when diseases were rife. Many members have urged him to take a holiday as he hasn't had a proper break for some time, an idea he regularly dismisses. Instead, he feels time is against him, and that he should have built the Metropolitan Tabernacle five years earlier. Because he is also in the last years of his ministry, he says he want to make the most of them.

He believes what the Scriptures say, "The King's business" requires haste. Not for him procrastination, rather pro-active involvement in everything he undertakes.

For example, from the official opening of the Tabernacle in 1994 until Christmas 1996, there was tremendous activity within the Whitewell church. A number of musicals for charity have taken place along with numerous Gospel missions, which show that the pastor has lost none of his zeal for preaching.

In one Gospel mission, over one hundred and forty people came to Christ.

There were other Gospel rallies throughout the province in towns like Ballymena, Omagh, Dungannon, Enniskillen, Armagh, and Newtownards, to name but a few. Hundreds of souls came to Christ at these missions as well as at the East Belfast Tent Mission in Mersey Street.

Despite the critics, the people still came - and how! Many of the new converts were young people. In fact 70% of the Whitewell congregation is under forty years of age. With no youth centre to house them, plans were drawn up and in just over a year a new sports complex was erected adjacent to the church. The estimated cost of this centre was £1 million, but, as in the construction of the Tabernacle, brethren of all ages worked round the clock lending their services free of charge, thus enabling the project to be completed at a cost of just £250,000.

Named "The Recreation Centre and Oasis Fitness Suite," it is open six days a week, and is on a par with many of the city's top leisure centres. It caters for 5-a-side football, volleyball, badminton, tennis and netball. On the first floor there is a bowling area, a selection of snooker tables, and table tennis facilities. Downstairs is a fitness suite complete with treadmill, cycle, step machine and full weights room.

It must be pointed out, however, that such a centre only exists today for one purpose: To help attract young men and women to the church in the hope that they will find the Lord Jesus Christ. They are the future generation and the reason the Metropolitan Tabernacle was considered in the first place.

---------------- ❖ ----------------

PART FOUR

AND THE GRACE OF GOD
WAS UPON HIM

---------------- ❖ ----------------

Chapter Twenty Eight

A MAN WITH A DIFFERENT SPIRIT

❖

Over the years James McConnell has displayed the faith of Abraham and Noah, the courage of Moses and Joshua, and the wisdom of Solomon; however, if he has resembled any Biblical character it is surely that of Caleb - the man the Bible says was of a different spirit.

Pastor McConnell's walk with God is not only a continual talking point among those who know him well, it is also overwhelming evidence of a life that has been fully surrendered to Christ. He exudes the one outstanding characteristic that belongs to all those who are chosen according to God's purpose - that of divine calling.

Divine calling, of course, is not just something that has been experienced by Biblical characters. Throughout the ages God has chosen man in the very same way. The chain of prophets has continued with, for example, Martin Luther, John Wesley, George Whitefield and Charles Spurgeon, to name but a few. These men are remembered not only for taking a stand, but also for inheriting outstanding individual characteristics which marked them out as having a different spirit.

In the case of James McConnell, spiritual revival in Ulster has been his appointed task, and recent years have brought about the realisation that if Ulster is to unite in Christian revival, then he and the Metropolitan Tabernacle will be very much a part of that revival.

From the beginning of the troubles he has earnestly contended that his mission is to play a part in bringing the two warring communities in Ulster together in love and peace through Christ.

Since moving to the Tabernacle, many people have asked why he has received such a blessing in his life. Words like faith, commitment, dedication and determination are all mentioned, but while all of these fit his description adequately, it's the word 'obedience' which may be the true reasons for that blessing.

Not just obedience in all aspects of the Christian life, however, but obedience to a command he received from the Holy Spirit some years ago. As he came into prominence in his ministry the Lord told him, "No matter what happens in your life, or despite how influential you may become, I do not want you to get involved in politics."

The Lord had another path for Pastor McConnell to tread - a path he has never veered from - the preaching of the gospel. He promised God that he would preach it faithfully and although he has had many opportunities to enter politics, he has always declined.

Indeed just prior to Christmas 1996, he announced, "I now know that I will never enter the political arena as God has helped me win far more souls for the Kingdom through preaching than I could ever have won had I been in politics."

Yet it could have been so easy to 'run with the crowd' or earn a good living outside of his church salary as a political representative, but as one local newspaper wrote shortly after the opening of the great Tabernacle:

"Pastor McConnell has found that God is the ultimate good employer."

He has been rewarded for his work far beyond his expectations. God told him all those years ago to go out and preach the gospel. The pastor did not ask for, nor did he seek, anything more.

He still takes a keen interest in the affairs of the land, however, and often expresses an opinion about the current state of his beloved Ulster.

Pastor McConnell is convinced that it is not the Catholic Church, nor the continuation of the troubles, which is hindering Christian revival in Ulster. Indeed it is the Protestant church which is the biggest obstacle. Their attitude, apathy and lack of imagination are all questionable.

It is this kind of bluntness which has set James McConnell apart from many others. It takes courage to stand alone, to proclaim the truth, even about your own people, but this servant of God has refused the offer of a life in politics and stuck rigidly to his task of preaching.

Having said this, one of the most dramatic sermons he has ever preached occurred just a year after the move to the Metropolitan Tabernacle in 1995 - a sermon which was aimed at the Roman Catholic Church.

Advertised in the Saturday edition of the Belfast Telegraph, the address was entitled: "Does the Roman Catholic Church worship Mary?"

Thousands turned up in response from every background, among them Roman Catholic priests and clergy. Extra chairs had to be brought into the Tabernacle that evening. If one considers that its capacity is four and a half thousand, it gives an indication of how much interest the subject generated.

As he stood at his pulpit, the pastor maintained that it was the Church of Rome and its doctrines that he was against, not the people of the Catholic Church. During that momentous evening he told the congregation:

"I know there are many sincere Catholics here tonight and in the Catholic Church. I want to tell you that I love all of you. I received your letters informing me that you don't worship Mary - and I believe you. But your Cardinals and Popes certainly do worship Mary and the Church of Rome fails miserably in this respect and falls miserably short of the Word of truth."

Despite receiving criticism afterwards, the reputation of the Tabernacle increased and numerous opportunities for him in civic life arrived with it. Yet he has remained true to his calling as a preacher of the gospel, with 'tunnel vision.' As it says of Caleb, "But my servant Caleb because he had a different spirit with him and hath followed me fully, him will I bring into the land where into he went; and his seed shall possess it." Numbers 14:24.

When Pastor McConnell was invited to sit on some of the province's most recognised committees between 1994 and 1996, he declined those invitations in order to concentrate fully on the ministry. The lure of a life in politics, though very strong at times, has never proven strong enough.

He agrees with the words of Joseph Parker who, after receiving similar invitations while pastoring the City Temple in London, commented, "I cannot be a politician and a pastor at the same time."

Like Parker, Pastor McConnell has no intention of wandering outside of what he describes as 'his own patch' - the Whitewell Metropolitan Tabernacle.

It's the place that has become his home - but, more importantly for him, it's the place where God wants him to be.

Chapter Twenty-Nine

THE UNIQUENESS OF THE MAN

---------------------- ❖ ----------------------

When the congregation of the Whitewell Metropolitan Tabernacle observe James McConnell in his role as pastor and preacher, it's here that they see the real uniqueness of the man.

From the beginning to the end of his services, he is a rare breed indeed.

For example, rain, hail or shine, every Sunday evening as various members and visitors arrive at the Tabernacle, they are greeted by the sight of the pastor helping to park the cars.

He doesn't need to do it, as there are already a number of attendants on duty. Today, of course, there are over three and a half thousand worshippers who attend on a Sunday evening but, as he sees it, that shouldn't make any difference to what has become for him, a life-long habit.

Many of his own congregation take this practice for granted, but not the visitors, who often comment on it. One lady who attended the Tabernacle for the first time was asked what she thought of the place.

"Not what I expected," she replied. When prompted further she added, "I expected to see the grand building and the large choir, but I never thought I would see the pastor helping to park the cars!"

Yet helping to park his parishioners' cars is just one of the many endearing actions he displays which marks his personality out as special. Not for him a grand entrance at the start of his services or a hasty retreat at the finish. He has always been a man of the people - a man who is committed to his flock, before, during, and after a service.

Certainly he has come a long way from that day when he knelt down in the little Bible Pattern Church and uttered the words, "Take my life and let it be, consecrated, Lord to Thee." It was a day when he experienced a true yielding to the Lord which, despite many trials and temptations since, has always endured.

The pastor's ministry hasn't always been without problems. In fact he has often brought trouble on himself by highly controversial statements he has made during his services. It's not a blot on his copybook, rather just the proof that he is flesh and blood. If he has something to say, he says it, and never attempts to dress it up.

Aside from this, the pastor is an unusual man, with many interesting traits. For example, he has never smoked a cigarette in his life, nor sipped a drop of alcohol, but he is full of sympathy for people who have problems with these two vices. "I think the greatest problem among new converts is smoking, acting as it does as a drug," says the pastor.

Over the years Pastor McConnell has tried to be patient with what he calls the 'smoking fraternity,' admitting that there have been quite a few believers who have found it difficult to stop smoking. Gladly he reports that many others who came to Christ at Whitewell have had victory over the habit and have been set gloriously free. He has pointed out to these converts that not only is smoking a dirty habit, but one that is going to kill them in the end. Eventually, after much prayer, Christ has delivered them.

He is surprised that, in his experience, people have been able to give up alcohol more quickly than cigarettes. Alcoholics, however, are a different story. He believes all ministers and Christians should be patient with alcoholics. He tells the story of one man in his church who suffered from the disease despite being a professing Christian.

"People used to telephone the church and tell me that this particular man was lying on the road and ask me what I was going to do about it. They would point out that the man was a member of the church and was letting down the people of God. I closed my eyes to it, as I knew he was crying for mercy and genuinely wanted deliverance from drink. Today he is free - a wonderful vessel for Christ - but it's worth stating that it took him well over two years to beat the habit."

The subject of whether or not Christians are allowed to smoke and drink has, of course, been debated many times. Some believers see nothing wrong with it. Ironically, they refer to the pastor's role model, C. H. Spurgeon, as a case in point. He was a man who smoked cigars and who drank alcoholic beverages. Others like John Wesley wouldn't drink tea, yet Wesley was said to be something of an authority on the taste of ale.

The pastor's personal opinion on this much-discussed subject is as follows: "I believe for me, as a Christian, it is wrong to smoke or to drink, but if other Christians choose to do this, I cannot judge them for it. After all, our Lord drank wine, while John the Baptist chose not to take any wine at all. One came neither eating nor drinking, and the Son of Man came eating and drinking, and yet they said both of them had a devil. Therefore I would leave the issue to the believer's personal choice."

His advice as a pastor is somewhat more defined. "Stop smoking and stop drinking and you will be much happier," he says.

Another controversial issue in Christian circles in recent years has been that of dancing, either in a hall or the church. Pastor McConnell is not an authority on the subject of dance-halls, due to the fact that he has never been in one.

The pastor is more comfortable about expressing an opinion on dancing within the church. He makes the point that

David danced before the Lord but not at every meeting with the Lord. He is not totally against dancing. It is the excessive dancing for no reason that he abhors. "There are churches where all they do is dance and nothing else," he says.

But despite his strong views on this he accepts that he blotted his own copybook by dancing at the conclusion of the East Belfast Tent Mission in 1996. The people were amazed, particularly from his own flock, when he began to dance openly before the Lord. One man said, "I have been with the pastor for 30 years and I have never seen anything like it." Another joked, "After that episode he will never again preach to me about dancing."

It was all extremely humorous and a performance that is never likely to be repeated. "So many people were getting saved, I couldn't resist it. Drug addicts,   alcoholics, Catholics, Protestants and paramilitaries were getting saved by the dozen so I just went mad," explains the pastor, without remorse. A lady who has been with the pastor from the days of the first church said, "Even when thousands were being saved at Windsor Park and the King's Hall during the 1980's, I don't remember him dancing like that ... he must be mellowing."

The dancing was just an outward expression of his love for the souls of men, but that different spirit he possesses has also given him a strong love for animals, particularly stray cats. His love affair with cats began some years ago when his daughter Julie persuaded him to buy a little cat for fifty pence, and he admits, "That cat became one of the most important persons in our home."

Called Darkie, the cat lived with the pastor for fourteen years until it took ill and died. Soon after this he was presented with six kittens, which he began to care for. This was followed by the arrival of another twelve and at one point he was responsible for feeding no fewer than eighteen cats. All of those animals are now dead, except one, but he says, "I still visit her four times a day to make sure she is well fed." He talks about this cat as if it were another member of his family. "She gets her breakfast at 7.30 am each morning, lunch at 1.00 pm, tea at 7.00 pm and supper at 10.00 pm" he says.

Recently in his life he has begun to unwind a little with the occasional game of snooker and with watching John Wayne movies. He still recalls how his father took him to see the American movie star in the cinema known as 'The Winkie'. He has a collection of John Wayne's greatest movies on video, but getting time to watch them isn't always easy.

Hundreds of people need advice each week, and despite having seven other pastors at their disposal, it seems that many of these needy souls prefer the services of Pastor McConnell. He copes with this by telling them that they will have to wait, due to his busy schedule.

"I have other men of God who are wonderful pastors and there is no need for me to be at every appointment," he says. That's not to say that he doesn't advise or visit members of his flock, especially in an emergency. They are his life and he is their pastor.

Chapter Thirty

STANDING FOR THE TRUTH

❖

An obvious requirement in expounding the Word of God is the need for preserving the balance of truth. Certainly that's a sentiment Pastor James McConnell agrees with fully. He continually urges his flock to adhere to the words of Second Timothy, 2:15, "Study to show thyself approved unto God, a workman that needeth not to be ashamed, rightly dividing the word of truth."

He has often emphasised that we are to 'rightly divide' the word of truth. "It's one thing knowing the scriptures, but knowing how to divide them is another."

During his own ministry Pastor James McConnell has been labelled a heretic despite displaying a consistently strong stance for the truth.

These accusations regarding heresy have never gone away during the course of his entire ministry. In fact, so persistent were they after the move to the new Tabernacle in 1994, that the pastor broke his own promise of not responding to slander by printing a full-colour brochure entitled, 'The Precious Word of Truth from the Metropolitan Tabernacle."

It was a move that was essential. He was concerned that the people who were making these insults were misleading many honest and hungry souls astray. He printed the booklet to ensure that every denomination would be left in no doubt as to what the people of Whitewell and their pastor stood for.

The brochure cost thousands of pounds to produce, but proved to be money well spent. He believes money is not important when it comes to saving someone's soul, especially as he has seen God meet every need of his own.

What then does Pastor James McConnell believe?

Firstly, he believes that the Bible is the infallible Word of God, fully inspired. It is the supreme and final authority in all matters of faith and conduct.

He further believes that mankind is totally depraved and because of that depravity he cannot save himself. Only an act of divine mercy and grace can save him. This alone comes from the Lord Jesus Christ.

He believes strongly in the efficacy and power of the shed blood of the Lord Jesus Christ to redeem and cleanse a man from his sin, and that all the just demands of a thrice Holy God have been satisfied because of the shed blood. No other remedy can wash a person from their sin.

He loves to sing the chorus, "Nothing but the blood of Jesus." In fact, after a Welshman attended the Tabernacle in 1996 and preached on the blood of Jesus, the pastor applauded and remarked, "You are welcome here any time if the blood of Jesus Christ is your theme."

As stated earlier, the pastor also believes fully in the Trinity and unity of the Godhead. Almighty God exists in three persons - the Father, the Son and the Holy Spirit.

As for the deity of Jesus Christ, he believes in His pre-existence in eternity as the Son of God who became the Son of Man. He is no less convinced about the miraculous conception of the Holy Ghost. He believes in the impeccable sinless life of Christ - living for us and keeping for us the law we could not keep - and in his substitutional and atoning death on Calvary, paying the full price God demanded for sin. How he loves to quote regularly the verse of scripture, "Behold the Lamb of God that taketh away the sin of the world." John 1:29.

There's no question over the accuracy of the resurrection in Pastor McConnell's ministry, either. He believes Christ rose again from the grave on the third day according to the scriptures and because He lives we shall live also. He extends this belief to the beautiful High Priestly ministry of Christ, Who stands bodily for us in the presence of God. Again his convictions are based on scripture, "For there is ONE God and ONE Mediator between God and men, the man Christ Jesus." I Timothy 2:5.

On the subject of eternal judgment the pastor believes in the punishment of the ungodly in the lake of fire, which the Lord Jesus mentions several times as "Hell Fire". This is the sole fate of the Christ rejector, "... knowing therefore the terror of the Lord we persuade men." II Corinthians 5:11.

He believes in the eternal conscious bliss of the redeemed and the eternal conscious punishment of the wicked. Pastor McConnell makes no apology for continually preaching about the subject of heaven and hell if there is to prevail a balance of truth.

Regarding the church, the pastor believes the true Church of Jesus Christ is made up of men and women from every nation under heaven, who have experienced the new birth and are indwelt by the Holy Spirit. And on the Holy Spirit he accepts the sovereignty and work of the Holy Spirit and baptism and fullness of the Holy Ghost. He believes totally in the gifts and graces right up to the present day and the ordinances of the Church such as the Lord's Day, the Lord's Supper and believer's baptism.

He is similarly convinced that divine healing according to scripture and the miraculous gifts recorded in the New Testament have never been taken out of the church. The pastor's reasons for this are based on experience. He has seen so many people healed and transformed by the power of the Holy Spirit during his lifetime that he cannot believe anything else.

It's during a Monday night prayer meeting at the Tabernacle that the Belfast pastor puts his faith to the test. Although he has often conceded that healing is not his ministry, it hasn't prevented many hundreds of people from various denominations receiving healing at those weekly prayer meetings. He literally lives out the words of James, "Is any sick among you? Let him call for the elders of the church, and let them pray over him, anointing him with oil in the name of the Lord. And the prayer of faith shall save the sick and the Lord shall raise him up: and if he have committed sins they shall be forgiven him." James 5:14,15.

The very fact that numerous members of the Tabernacle have been witnesses to the authenticity of this kind of healing is proof for the pastor that, if you have faith in God's Son, anything is possible.

Of course, to overcome difficulties in life such as trials and temptations, sickness, loneliness, bereavement, debt or despair, we all need to have faith - but what kind of faith? 1 John 5:4 says, "For whatsoever is born of God overcometh the world and this is the victory that overcometh the world, even our faith."

True faith is when we accept Jesus Christ as our personal Saviour and believe in God to provide for every aspect of our lives.

That has been the story of Pastor James McConnell's entire life. During his youth he had nothing, but believed God for something. His early years at Whitewell were a testimony to this. In those days he possessed little, but still he believed God for much ... and much has certainly materialised.

But it has taken supreme faith in God to bring about the building of a work as huge as the Metropolitan Tabernacle in Belfast, and it has also meant great sacrifice.

So to ensure fully that they would be recognised as a church which preached God's Word in its entirety, the Metropolitan Tabernacle has, in recent years, become affiliated to the Elim Pentecostal Church in Great Britain and Ireland. The fact that Pastor James McConnell's assembly is part of such an organisation proves it has been accepted as one which stands for the truth of Holy Scripture.

The fellowship that Pastor McConnell has enjoyed has become very precious to him and he has shared in gospel crusades with Elim leaders.

The pentecostal church is the fastest growing denomination on earth, therefore the pastor sees the increase in numbers at the Tabernacle as confirmation of this.

Yet such an increase is surely a tribute to the pastor's own standing for the faith. From childhood he has been brought up with strong pentecostal beliefs such as spiritual gifts, speaking in tongues, divine healing and the supernatural element. He is a traditionalist in his thinking, Calvinistic in his theology, and historical, not futuristic, in his interpretation of Bible prophecy. Above all, though, he is very much a fundamentalist in his Christian walk.

While the increase in attendances at weekly worship within pentecostal assemblies is of great encouragement to the pastor, he is not so optimistic about the growth of many of the other evangelical denominations.

On the contrary, he is quite critical of them. He believes they are fossilising in a generation when they should be moving forward with great vision.

People are critical of him because hundreds have come out of their denominational churches to attend the Tabernacle, but the pastor believes that is primarily because they are not being fed the gospel of truth in their respective churches.

Pastor McConnell has no other secret than preaching Jesus Christ and Him crucified - and refuses to listen to any other standard of truth.

The pastor feels many evangelicals have failed in their faithfulness to the truth. He accepts that preaching other things is good, but believes that the preaching of the Gospel is the best.

He accuses ministers who don't preach about the cross as being the enemies of God. This opinion is based on scripture where Paul declares, "For many walk of whom I have told you often, and now tell you even weeping, that they are the enemies of the cross of Christ." Phil. 3:18.

These statements from Pastor McConnell are nothing new. In fact, it is this kind of honesty and frankness which has often caused commotion within the evangelical community in Ulster, particularly in recent years. Many agree with his sentiments, but just as many others, if not more, have taken exception to his comments and have let him know in no uncertain terms.

He continues undeterred, true to his calling, which he says is as a 'Minister of the truth.' Christ didn't call him to be the friend of everyone, he called him to preach the truth to everyone.

These days as thousands converge on the Tabernacle, the pastor is often nervous before preaching his sermons as he is well aware that many have come to scrutinise him. Once he has said his opening prayer, however, he tends to forget about his fears and goes on with the preaching of the Gospel - or the preaching of what he calls, "the old message, touched with the power of the Holy Ghost."

Nevertheless such a belief has cost the pastor dearly over the years in that he has lost some of his best friends and colleagues. He has been urged many times to follow 'the popular path' but he has reluctantly parted company with those who have made these suggestions.

To use an appropriate term in Ulster, they wanted him to decommission from the truth, but he has stuck to his convictions and refused to decommission.

Some years ago Pastor McConnell's fundamentalist approach was sneered at on the arrival of what many believe were 'religious cults'. In recent years, however, such an approach has been well and truly justified as his stand for the truth has waxed stronger and stronger.

Indeed, Pastor McConnell has continued to preach the truth, despite the emergence of "new things" such as different forms of worship. Preaching faithfully in the old Orange Hall he prophesied that such a trend would develop if men of God left their posts. Sadly, he says, this has come to pass.

For him, it's always been the old things, the old landmarks - and nothing less than the blood of Jesus.

In the words of Paul the apostle ... 'For I determined not to know anything among you, save Jesus Christ, and Him crucified.' I Corinthians 2:2.

Chapter Thirty-One

THE PROVIDENCE OF CHRIST

---------------------- ❖ ----------------------

No one is immune from the storms of life - a life that offers the glittering sunlight of summer, but also produces the piercing chill of winter. There are days of overwhelming joy, but there are also days of unutterable sorrow. How especially true this is of men who serve in the ministry.

The life of James McConnell has been no exception. He has experienced tragedy on the one hand and blessing on the other.

Remember how he lost his parents at a tender age which left him feeling unwanted and alone. How he grew up poor materially and, to some extent, uneducated. Being rejected by his peers during the ministry, despite standing for the truth, and having to face numerous disappointments during his vocation at Whitewell, are other examples of tragic consequences in his life.

Blessings have come, too. For example, the marriage to his faithful wife, Margaret, and the joy of seeing his daughter Linda surrender her life to Christ.

Through it all, however, James has continued to serve the Lord with great fervency. Despite chalking up over forty years of service in God's work, this Belfast pastor has the same zeal today, if not more than ever, for his calling.

The Metropolitan Tabernacle, Belfast, is the crowning of his life. Yet its success is a far cry from the days when he grew up as a little boy in East Belfast. Amidst the greatest storms of his life he quickly found that God doesn't bring us out of them. He brings us through them.

During his youth, as James was waiting for God to build a bridge over his troubled waters, God in turn was waiting for James to take on a life jacket of faith.

Yet his Captain Jesus Christ didn't expect his servant to make that journey without some form of encouragement.

The first promise the Lord made to James was to provide for his every need through His great providence.

The same Jesus who sent His disciples out on a boat to be met by a great storm, also planned a stormy upbringing for his servant James McConnell, and while it is fair to say that many storms are caused through Christians disobeying God (for example, Jonah was so far away from God's will that he found himself inside the belly of the whale and caught in a storm of correction) James hadn't done anything wrong. The problems he endured during his youth were endured while he was obeying the Lord so this wasn't a storm of correction. It was a storm of perfection.

How else could he have explained losing both his parents when he was a young man, or being brought up by godly grandparents who introduced him to the things of God. Significant, too, was the fact that while friends and relatives were dying due to serious illnesses, James experienced full health.

The truth was that, but for the providential intervention of a mighty God, there simply wasn't any other explanation for the events in his life at that time.

The grace of God rested upon him even as a young boy, although realising and even believing this, must have been difficult. As is the case today, God's Word was his reassurance.

For example, it was in the storms of sorrow and tears that the prophecies of Jeremiah emerged. It was in a storm of infertility that Hannah became a godly woman. It was in the storm of exile on the Isle of Patmos that John saw and recorded the magnificent visions of the Book of Revelation. It was in storms of adversity that Saul became the blazing apostle Paul.

During his own storms, James sought constantly the assurance that he wasn't outside, but inside, the will of God.

Back in those early days in Spring Street it seemed all was tragic in his life, and it was.

Without the proper care of a mum and dad for most of his childhood, he couldn't have wished for a worse start in life. But, think about it:

If he hadn't been brought up by the example of his godly grandfather, he may never have known God.

If he hadn't suffered great loneliness back then, he may never have identified fully with the suffering and loneliness of Christ.

If he hadn't identified fully with those sufferings, he may never have exuded the fire and brimstone in his preaching which he has become renowned for.

If he hadn't experienced an unstable upbringing he may never have met pastors James Forsythe and Gordon Magee.

If he hadn't met these two men, he would not have had the proper training for the ministry.

If he hadn't that training, he could not have become such a dynamic preacher.

If he hadn't become such a prolific preacher, there would have been no such place as the Metropolitan Tabernacle.

If there had been no such place as the Metropolitan Tabernacle, thousands of souls would not have come to Christ through his ministry.

Remarkably, instead of going down, God was bringing him up.

Like Joseph, who was sold as a slave into Egypt, the pastor may have looked dead and buried, but he found out later that he was in the centre of God's will. He was only in the pit temporarily. The palace was on its way.

Oh, yes, he was living in a storm in those early days, but it was a storm of true perfection, allowed by Almighty God. Those storms have continued since in the life of James McConnell. He has over the years suffered rejection and loneliness and has been hurt many times, sadly in some instances by professing Christians.

The lesson here, however, is surely that God whispers to us in our pleasures, but shouts to us in our pain. And there are some things that can never happen to us without great suffering first.

Chapter Thirty-Two

THE PRAYERS OF CHRIST

❖

Remember how Christ sent the multitudes away and went up to the mountain to pray. The Bible says, "And when he had sent them away, he departed into a mountain to pray" Mark 6:46.

What a blending of the deity and humanity of Christ this is. That very afternoon Jesus, as God, had fed the five thousand. At evening time He, as man, stood and prayed. When the disciples went out to sea, Jesus went out to pray.

God was well aware that James McConnell was struggling against his own boisterous sea and even in those dark hours during his childhood and later in his ministry, Christ fully comprehended the pastor's need of prayer.

Hanging on the wall of the Metropolitan Tabernacle, Belfast, is the text, "Jesus Christ, the same yesterday, today and forever." Hebrews 13:8.

The pastor has no doubt that the same Jesus who prayed for His disciples during their storm, is the same Jesus who has stood and prayed for him.

There have been many times when the pastor's back has been against the wall of adversity, not only during his childhood but later on as the pastor of the Whitewell Church. Yet Christ has gone into the presence of God and made intercession for James.

The pastor has often told his assembly to pray for him and for the great work at the Tabernacle, but how much more comforting it has been for him to know that Christ was personally praying for him.

Often at the Sunday morning Breaking of Bread services the pastor quotes, "To know that the King of kings and Lord of lords is praying for me in the glory; to know that my Lord and Saviour Jesus Christ is standing praying for me, is my greatest comfort."

Again there is a lesson in all of this. Whatever our battles or struggles, there is one who is praying for us. No matter what the devil tells the Father about us, Christ is there to plead our case and remind the Father that we are covered by His precious blood.

That's not to say that the pastor refuses to pray. For him, prayer is as essential as breakfast, lunch and tea. He is thankful that Christ prays for us, but he believes we also need to pray to God.

That's true if we consider that when Jesus walked on the sea he would have passed by the disciples, but for one reason. They called out to Him for help.

The Bible says, "And when they saw Him walking on the sea they supposed it had been a spirit, and cried out ..." Mark 6: 49.

This is what the pastor of the Metropolitan Church and his congregation have made a lifetime habit - crying out to God for help. When his own storms arrived, the pastor has called upon the Master of the seas of life and He has answered in the same way as He answered the disciples. "He saith unto them, be of good cheer, be not afraid, it is I." Mark 6: 50. How relieved, on many occasions, James McConnell has been on hearing the words, "It is I."

Mind you, there have been times when he didn't feel like praying, but this pastor has prayed anyway. Spurgeon once commented, "Groanings which cannot be uttered are often prayers which cannot be refused." For those seeking the real reason behind the success of the Metropolitan Tabernacle, here is the answer. Prayer and prayer alone.

Seven prayer meetings every week of every year appear to have impressed Almighty God, for He has answered so many of those prayers in different ways. It hasn't always been easy to believe, though.

Like the disciples, there have been many times in the life of James McConnell when Christ has told the wind and waves to be still. Equally, there have been many other occasions when Christ remained completely silent. He was nowhere to be found.

Like all of us, James has had to endure those times in life that were not easy to understand, but significantly the prayers of Christ and the pastor's own prayers have helped considerably.

Back in those early days of the Orange Hall when he had just 30 or 40 members and multiple problems, he would earnestly ask:

"Where are you, Lord?" Christ would answer, "I'm praying for you."

When he believed God would meet the huge financial needs of his ministry, though nothing seemed to happen, again he would cry in the privacy of his home:

"Where are you, Lord?" Again the Lord would say, "I'm praying for you."

When Pastor McConnell cried unto God to come and bring peace to the nation of Ulster, but the bombings and killings continued, he groaned from the depths of his soul the same words of the disciples when they were being tossed to and fro on the sea of Galilee:

"Where are you Lord?" The only answer he got was, "I'm praying for you."

There must have been days when the pastor almost stopped. Almost gave up. He didn't though and God came through for him. Christ answered those prayers and answered in his own good time.

What a shame that when many of us are faced with a personal storm we consult with pastors, deacons, friends and family, but never actually talk to the Lord Jesus Christ, the one who has the power to change every situation.

That's never been the case in the life of Pastor James McConnell. Jesus Christ may have been praying for him, but he has always prayed for others.

Chapter Thirty-Three

THE PRESENCE OF CHRIST

❖

A sk any visitor who comes to the Metropolitan Tabernacle for their reaction and afterwards most of them end up confessing how they felt the presence of God not only in the building but also with the pastor.

That presence has been with Pastor McConnell since he knelt down at an old bench in the Iron Hall at just seven years of age, but in recent years it has become even more apparent.

For example, as he comes down from the platform on Sunday mornings to meet his people before breaking bread, his face is often glowing due to the presence of God. Such a blessing doesn't come naturally. He spends hours walking and talking with his Saviour. Over the hills of Cavehill, near his home, or walking along the busy streets, he hungers and thirsts after righteousness.

At one of his prayer meetings in 1996, the pastor asked his congregation, "Have you ever seen the face of an angel?" He answered his own question with the words, "It's beautiful."

Although reluctant to talk about his own experiences with the Angel of the Lord, there can be little doubt that such visitations have left a great mark on the pastor. He is a walking example of the text, "And they looked unto Him, and were lightened: and their faces were not ashamed." Psalm 34:5.

The presence of God in his life is obvious, but so too is the consistency of his ministry. Rarely does he approach his people with a negative spirit. He is always on a high. Always ablaze for God.

How does he constantly hide any difficulties in his life and produce such a witness in front of his own assembly? It is through experience and through the Holy Spirit. Those are the main reasons for his continual joy.

Back in those difficult days of pastoring and witnessing on the Whitewell Road, gun battles were raging, his church and his buses were being set on fire, and no one wanted to come to his church as he was regarded by many as a 'ministerial fake'.

In the light of all this it would have been so easy for James to have become discouraged - and even to have given up. We now know, however, that those were the days when God moved in a mighty way.

Here is another wonderful lesson about the gift of true faith: when the pastor thought Christ wasn't going to turn up, the same Jesus appeared and supplied every need. The troubles eased, the people arrived, and the money poured in to help him accomplish a great work for God in the shape of the Metropolitan Tabernacle.

Yet wasn't such a presence also with the disciples on the boat? It was at the darkest hour, known as "the fourth watch" or the middle of the night, that Jesus appeared to them, walking on the water. It was just when they thought the Lord wasn't going to appear that he arrived and met their need.

Christ has met the need of Pastor McConnell in the same way.

These days thousands are attending Pastor McConnell's church. At the Christmas musical in 1996, hundreds were turned away as there was no room for them either in the church or in the car park.

A wonderful achievement, but the pastor's desire to have the presence of God with him has always been even greater than other holy ambitions.

Many marvel at the beautiful building, but they marvel equally at what God has done with this ordinary man.

On his ever increasing love for Christ, Pastor McConnell says, "The longer I serve Him, the sweeter He grows." And you know he means it.

His style these days is homespun Belfast. He has a bantering rapport with his congregation, but the presence of God is never far away. More and more he preaches without apparent reference to notes. As he does so, young and old focus on him, thumbing through their Bibles.

"Say, 'Praise the Lord'" he tells them, in one of his best known phrases.

"Praise the Lord," they reply.

Following the biggest service of the week - on Sunday evening - hundreds file out into the foyer, past the rockery-style fountain, out into the car park, many being unaware of just how much God has blessed the Whitewell ministry. Northern Ireland's evening newspaper, the Belfast Telegraph, reported after the official opening of the Tabernacle that "such a car park would do justice to any out-of-town shopping centre."

Today the car park is too small - a wonderful reminder, in a way, of what God has done through this Belfast pastor. James now desperately requires adequate parking facilities for the church and, as well as that, he also needs a lift to accommodate pensioners who cannot manage the stairs.

As the pastor waxes stronger and stronger, it's hard to comprehend that he is the same man who has endured so much personal tragedy.

Perhaps someone reading this today is hurting. Maybe you are going through persecution, rejection, loneliness, sorrow and suffering of great magnitude. Maybe you have picked up this book in a final bid to receive a word from God. You may be a pastor or a preacher. As someone once asked:

"Who does the pastor talk to when things are going badly?"

You may have tried everything, even positive thinking, but all has failed. You know in your heart that you need to hear from God and God alone.

Surely the story of the twelve disciples out on the boat, caught in the heat of the battle but gloriously delivered by their Saviour, will tell you that it's too soon to give up.

Surely an appreciation of the life of this Belfast pastor, two thousand years on from the ministry of Christ, will encourage you not to quit. If Jesus is the same yesterday, today and forever, why not call out to Him while there is still time to be rescued?

As Pastor McConnell himself often quotes, "God's delays are not always His denials."

Hang in, believe God and endure to the end. This has been the life conviction of Pastor James McConnell. He shepherded just forty people for almost twelve years. That is not success in anyone's book. He kept going, though, and look what God has done.

To persevere when the world is against you takes courage and great faith.

There can be no doubt that the life of James McConnell has been a great testimony of courage and faith, of persevering until the end, and hoping. As the Bible says, "But without faith it is impossible to please Him: for he that cometh to God must believe that he is and that He is a rewarder of them that diligently seek Him." Hebrews 11:6.

Throughout his own lifetime the pastor has walked the Word of God by faith, not by sight, and the results have been astounding.

How blessed his life has been due to the providence, prayers and the presence of Almighty God. His only desire has been to preach the gospel and lift up the name of Jesus Christ at every opportunity.

"Say, Praise the Lord!"

The Woman Who Dreamed About Christ

A Message Preached in the
Whitewell Metropolitan Tabernacle
by Dr. James McConnell

THE WOMAN WHO DREAMED
ABOUT CHRIST

❖

Scripture Reading: Matthew 27:15-26

Men of science are sometimes able to reconstruct the shape and size of a completely extinct species from a single bone or splinter of a bone that has been quite accidentally dug out of the earth ...

And in something of the same way, the wife of Pontius Pilate rises up before us out of a single sentence in Matthew's gospel. We see the governor's wife only for a moment, we hear her only for a moment but in the space of that short moment in time she so impresses her sudden footprint that, as long as Matthew's gospel is read, what Pilate's wife said and did that Passover morning will be held in an honourable remembrance of her. For this woman openly and sincerely acknowledged the innocence of our Lord Jesus Christ.

Just what form her dream took that Passover night, I would give a lot to know. The Scriptures are silent concerning it but they are not silent concerning her reaction to that dream. Whatever happened in the night watches shook her to her very soul.

In her dream she may have seen the Son of Man coming in His glory with all the holy angels with him ...

She may have seen the kings of the earth and the great men and the rich men and the mighty men, with her husband among them, hiding themselves in the dens and rocks of the mountains, crying, "Fall on us and hide us from the face of Him that sitteth on the Throne" ...

She might have seen a hand coming out and writing on the wall of the Praetorian like Belshazzar saw - "Thou art weighed in the balances and found wanting" ...

She might have seen her own husband who, on the following day, would call to the multitude- "What shall I do then with Jesus which is called Christ?" Standing in a future day, his hands soaked with blood which a thousand basins of water could not wash off, before a great white throne, wailing, "What shall he do with me?"

No wonder the message was sent in haste - "Have nothing to do with that just man, for I have suffered many things this day in a dream because of Him."

At first sight perhaps this short passage of Scripture would seem to have no hidden meaning but when we take it word by word we learn a number of things:

Firstly, it suggests - the judgment hall in which Christ was condemned lay some distance from Pilate's residence. Otherwise surely the wife would come herself with her urgent petition.

Secondly, the trial must have taken place very early and Pilate must have left government house before his wife was awake.

Thirdly, Pilate and his wife must have seriously discussed Jesus before the night of the arrest in the garden of Gethsemane because the urgency of her message shows a keen appreciation of the danger in which he stood.

Maybe at the beginning of the trial of Jesus, Pilate was going to treat it as just another case - he despised the Jews, he despised their priests, he despised their customs and their hypocrisy. But before the trial was over, coupled with this sinister warning from his wife, Pilate knew he was dealing with something and somebody which was too big for him, too big for his superior Tiberias Caesar and too big for the mighty Roman Empire.

He was dealing with destiny and with deity and he was a small cog in that great wheel but nevertheless he was playing his part. Is it any wonder the Scripture says "It is a fearful thing to fall into the hands of the living God."

I believe there comes a time in every man's life when eternal issues stare him in the face, issues like death, judgment and mercy.

It seems Jesus Christ, who was God manifest in flesh, was in the hands of the Roman Governor ... Pilate was Caesar's representative in Judea, he alone could decide what a man's fate was. But little did Pilate know it was all decided away back in the regions of eternity, before Adam was planted in the Garden of Eden.

When Jesus answered nothing to the accusations of the priest, Pilate marvelled at Christ's silence. He cried, "Do you not know I have power to crucify thee and power to release thee?" The answer Jesus gave him rocked him to his foundations ... He said, "Thou couldst have no power at all against me except it were given thee from above, therefore he (meaning Caiaphas, the High Priest) that delivered me unto thee, hath the greater sin". The Apostle Peter, on the Day of Pentecost, preached this to the people gathered round the Upper Room. He said, "Jesus of Nazareth, a man approved of God among you by miracles and wonders and signs, which God did by Him in the midst of you as ye yourselves know: Him, being delivered by the determinate counsel and foreknowledge of God, ye have taken and by wicked hands have crucified and slain". That day as Jesus stood before Pilate, it was a question - who was in the hands of who?

Pilate's wife must have realised, pagan and all as she was, that her husband was like Belshazzar, King of the Chaldeans, in the hands of the living God - "Have nothing to do with that just man, for I have suffered many things this day in a dream because of Him."

"WHO WAS PILATE'S WIFE?"

Who was Pilate's wife? There is an air of mystery about her that has made the Bible student probe for the smallest piece of information concerning her ... Tradition claims that her name was Claudia Procula and she may well have belonged to the Claudia Gems who were one of the richest and most powerful families in Rome. She is said to have been a granddaughter of the Emperor Augustus and if this were so it explains why Pilate was able to break the rule that forbade provincial governors to take their wives with them to the provinces. It is probable that both by birth and connection she was of higher rank than her husband and that Pilate's important post in Judea was due to her influence. As wife of the Roman Governor, Claudia would have lived in the surroundings of a Queen. Reading all the history I could get on Pilate and his wife, I came to the conclusion that Claudia was a beautiful and intelligent woman and Pilate was most fortunate to have her by his side. She was too good a "help meet" to leave behind at Rome. Claudia shared all her husband's anxieties, all his responsibilities, all his apprehensions in one of the most rebellious provinces in the Roman Empire - Judea! But little did she know that at the Feast of the Passover she and her husband were going to share also in the greatest farce of justice the history of law has ever known - the trial and murder of the Lord Jesus Christ!

Some Bible commentators, however, are very kind to Claudia. They build a lot of supposition around her because of her dream about the Lord Jesus ... They say she believed Jesus was a just man (that's true, she said that) and some of them feel the message she sent to Pilate was a plea to save the life of Jesus (that point is debatable). So taking these theories altogether they have Claudia among the first Romans of the Gentiles who accepted Jesus Christ as their Saviour. Paul, in his epistle to Timothy, mentions a "Claudia" and some commentators say that she was Pilate's wife. If this were true it would be wonderful but it's too vague, it's too dark, it's too much enshrouded in mystery; it should be out in the open where everybody can see and know it. I personally would rather base my facts on what the Scriptures say than on wishful thinking! What do the Scriptures say? Matthew says Claudia dreamed a dream.

God can speak to the human soul in many ways. One of those ways can be through a dream ...

It is not the first time God has spoken and revealed Himself in a dream and I'm sure it will not be the last ... Many times in scripture, to protect men, to direct men and counsel men, God appeared to them in a dream. Men like Abraham, Jacob, Joseph, Solomon, Pharaoh and Nebuchadnezzar. In the New Testament, to such men as Peter, Paul and John, but in our story tonight God revealed Himself to a woman, a pagan, a Roman - Pilate's wife.

The Romans were great believers in dreams. They put much store by them and God knowing this used this means of warning Pilate and his wife of the awful danger they were in.

Now, I don't know what sort of idea you have about God? Maybe God to you is an austere being, remote, distant, isolated, locked in Heaven somewhere, disappointed in humanity. So disappointed He doesn't care or bother with us any more. That's a wrong idea, my friend. The very fact that he moved upon a woman's subconscious mind in her sleep, to transmit to her soul a warning of damnation that could affect her for all eternity, shows that God isn't remote and isolated at all, but very concerned that men and women should discover Him and have eternal life. The apostle Peter reinforces this argument when he said, "The Lord is long suffering, not willing that any should perish but that all should come to repentance."

God is a God of judgment, a God of righteous judgment, never forget this! But He is also a God of love and, had Pilate and his wife only realised it, God in His great love and mercy was offering them salvation and a knowledge that the man brought before them was a just man and different to any other man in the world.

It seemed Pilate, with the warning of this dream sent by his wife, was going to accept what God had offered them because he openly declared to the multitude, "Behold, I bring Him forth to you that ye may know that I find no fault in Him." But ladies and gentlemen, it didn't work out that way, as we shall see!

"HAVE NOTHING TO DO WITH HIM"

Now we have noted from the Scriptures that Claudia dreamed a dream, a dream that had greatly distressed her but also had convinced her that the prisoner at the bar was a just man. Some commentators, I feel at this juncture, have allowed themselves to be carried away by this confession of Christ's innocence ... and they read between the lines of this confession that the message she sent to Pilate was a plea to save Jesus's life. I must admit that I too was tempted to read between the lines but we don't need to. All that God wants us to see in this verse is here right before us. What was her message? "Have nothing to do with that just man for I have suffered many things this day in a dream because of Him." Notice, Pilate's wife did not say, save Him! She said, "Have nothing to do with him" and that indeed was Pilate's intention. He, too, like his wife believed Jesus was a just man but Caiaphas and Annas the High Priests had brought the prisoner to him that he might judge him. Claudia's advice to have nothing to do with Him wasn't as easy as it sounded.

What's the charge against the prisoner? (asks Pilate). Caiaphas, the High Priest, replies, "We found this fellow perverting the nation and forbidding to give tribute to Caesar saying that He himself is Christ a King." Pilate looks and examines the accused. He turns to the Chief Priests and the people - "I find no fault in this man." The multitude explodes in anger. They shout back, "This man stirreth up the people teaching them through all our Jewry, beginning from Galilee to this place ..." Pilate is exasperated but a light comes into his eye and the word that puts this light into his eye is Galilee! He says to himself, if this man is from Galilee he doesn't come under my jurisdiction at all but that of Herod Antipas (the murderer of John the Baptist). Fortunately Herod is in Jerusalem for the Feast of the Passover. Pilate heaves a sigh of relief - I'm saved, I've found a legitimate means of satisfying my wife and relieving myself of a most uncomfortable position.

Not only that, I'll gain favour with the Jews by leaving the final decision to one of themselves and at the same time I will be hitting old Herod who hates me and has been spying on me and sending bad reports to Tiberias Caesar concerning me. Without loss of time Pilate orders his soldiers to take Jesus to the man who beheaded John the Baptist.

It didn't work out the way Pilate thought it would. The murderer of John the Baptist was glad to see Jesus, hearing so many things about Him and hoping that he might see a miracle done by Him. He mocked Him and his soldiers sported about Him but Herod didn't lay a finger on Him because he was afraid "this was John the Baptist risen from the dead". The sad thing was, Christ had not one single word to say to Herod Antipas. The night John's head was severed from his body, God the Holy Ghost was finished with Herod. Ladies and gentlemen - Herod, though living, was lost before he entered into the caverns of the damned.

Can you imagine Pilate's face when Caiaphas and his mob brought the Saviour, who was utterly exhausted, back to him again? Oh! Claudia, your advice is not as easy as it sounds, "Have nothing to do with Him". That man Caiaphas and his breed are determined that I will have everything to do with Him. How many people have tried the same tactic of neutrality that Pilate tried? I'll tell you - millions! But it's impossible. Sooner or later, my friend, you'll come into contact with Jesus Christ and when you do you must tell Him whose side you're on.

There are some issues in life when one can sit on the fence and be neutral but in the greatest issue of life - the personal salvation of your soul - you can't be in between, you must be for Jesus Christ or against Him. Your eternal destiny rests on it. It is impossible to be neutral in this great matter of salvation. God will never accept neutrality concerning His Son, to be neutral is to be lost. The statement Jesus made to His disciples 1900 years ago is still valid for today … "He that is not with me is against me; and he that gathereth not with me scattereth abroad." (Matthew 12:30).

Some time ago I found myself in a company of men, when to my surprise the conversation arose concerning the character of Pontious Pilate. One of the men said, "You can't but help pity Pilate." Yes, I replied, I pitied Pilate, but I also despised him. Pilate was a coward and he should have stuck to his verdict but he changed it for pride of face, pride of place, to gain favour with the people." And there are thousands of people like him (they'll sell their principles and their convictions for position and an extra £1 in their stipend.) Friend, it's better to lose your position and your prestige than to lose your soul.

The sad thing about Pilate is, in the end, he did lose his position and prestige. His behaviour after the crucifixion was so bad that Caesar sent for him and banished him to Gaul. But the shadow of the Galilean Carpenter whose murder he sanctioned went with him. A broken Pilate committed suicide and tonight he awaits the judgment of the one he had condemned.

Before Pilate released Jesus for crucifixion he did a thing to try and ease his conscience and to please his distressed wife Claudia. He took a basin of water and washed his hands publicly before the multitude. He said, "I am innocent of the blood of this just person, see ye to it." Poor Pilate, what nonsense was this. To condemn Jesus and yet protest that he was innocent of His blood. For men to protest against an act and yet to put into practice that very act is only proof that they are sinning against their own conscience. He said to the priest and the people, "See ye to it." It's your responsibility now, not mine, and to his surprise the Jewish nation said, (and take note) "Then answered all the people His blood be upon us and on our children."

This reminds me that when Judas Iscariot, realising the enormity of his sin, went back to the Chief Priests with the thirty pieces of silver they had bargained with, he said, "I have sinned in that I have betrayed the innocent blood!" They sneered, "What is that to us? See thou to it." Pilate, handing Jesus over to them, said the same thing, "See thou to it."

Old Matthew Henry was right. He said, "Sin is a brat that nobody is willing to own." Many deceive themselves that they will bear no blame so long as they can find somebody to lay the blame on. But guilt, ladies and gentlemen, is not as easy a thing to transfer as we may think.

Have thou nothing to do with that just man! That's impossible - because He died, the just for the unjust, that He might bring us to God.